The *Ultimate*
BULK BUYING
Cookbook

120 Money Saving, Family Pleasing Recipes

Jan Muller and Bob Warden

Published by **DYNAMIC** HOUSEWARES INC

First paperback edition 2010

10 9 8 7 6 5 4 3 2

For information about special discounts for bulk purchases
please contact sales@dynamichousewares.com

Authors: Jan Muller and Bob Warden

Food Styling and Photographs: Carole Haffey

Book Design: Christian and Elise Stella

Copy Editor: Kelly Machamer

Manufactured in the USA

ISBN 978-0-9841887-4-1

contents

Jan Muller

INTRODUCTION

Yes, it's true! You really can save thousands of dollars a year by buying most of your groceries in bulk packages or large 'family packs' at a wholesale warehouse club or your neighborhood grocery store. Warehouse clubs offer every item in bulk packaging, and they typically offer large assortments of beef, poultry, pork, lamb, and assorted seafood. Nowadays, more and more grocery chains are also increasing their bulk family pack selections as customer demand for money saving options grows every year.

This book is written for both the veteran warehouse club shopper and for those just getting started down the path to savings. We've combined our knowledge of bulk shopping (a total of over 50 years!) to help you take advantage of these huge savings. Since we first introduced the FoodSaver® on television 25 years ago, we've seen that the average across-the-board savings of buying in bulk has kept steady at about 40% of the total annual grocery bill. You can save well over a thousand dollars a year, just on your meat and seafood purchases alone.

Packaged, bottled, and canned groceries are an easy bulk purchase; you just put the extra packs, bottles, and cans in your pantry and use them when needed. However, bulk packs of perishable fresh meat and fish can be more intimidating. That's where a home vacuum sealer and a home freezer can come in handy. In this book, we'll show you how to turn every bulk meat or fish purchase into several delicious and simple to prepare family meals.

You may be surprised to find that the recipes in this book are for normal, family-sized meals. This book is not about making one dish out of an entire bulk package of meat that could feed over a dozen people. This book is about providing you with several different recipes for that type of meat, so that you can split, separate, and prepare several unique meals from one bulk package. You might cut an 8 pound pork loin into two family-sized roasts and half a dozen pork chops to prepare into 3 separate dinners, vacuum sealing and freezing the portioned meat until you feel like making one of the pork recipes in this book. While you won't be cooking the entire bulk package in one meal, there's no need to worry; these recipes are hearty, and there will still be plenty of leftovers to seal, freeze, and reheat another day!

Many of the recipes in this book also include tips on how to seal and reheat the final dish. With these tips you may choose to prepare multiple meals in one day—sealing and freezing for a stockpile of dinners that can be easily reheated anytime you need them, even at a moment's notice. We've known many working individuals who put aside one day of their weekend to prepare, seal, and store their family's meals for the entire work week.

Bob Warden

Source: Consumer Reports Shopsmart Magazine
November 2009

Whether you choose to separate and seal your bulk purchases raw for later preparation—or to separate, prepare, and seal finished meals for later consumption—this book will fit in perfectly with your plans. You will never have to pass up a bulk package of inexpensive chicken thighs just because you are unsure of how you could possibly use it all. Now, you will know immediately that you can turn that package into three or four meals simply by turning to page 107 in this book and choosing from the ten recipes in the Chicken Thighs and Legs category.

Though it should be obvious by now that we have been avidly vacuum sealing food for decades, we do understand that the desire to save money is universal—that there will be many people without vacuum sealers who are also intrested in bulk shopping to prepare the recipes in this book.

You do not need a vacuum sealer in order to bulk shop or prepare the recipes in this book, as we do not wish to discourage anyone from saving money for their family! Many of the recipes in this book suggest vacuum sealing before marinating a cut of meat—which really gets the marinade deep into the meat for the most tender results—but if you do not own a vacuum sealer, simply marinate in a covered dish. Other than that, you should be able to use all of our recipes in this book as is. And after you've made it through your first few weeks of bulk shopping, we'd highly recommend putting some of the

savings you've made toward a home vacuum sealer to fully protect your bulk purchases from going bad or getting freezer burnt.

We've found that the twenty-three cuts of beef, poultry, pork, lamb, and fish presented in this book are the most popular and readily available in bulk at warehouse clubs. Many of these are also available in family packs at your neighborhood grocery store. In separate sections devoted to each cut, we'll tell you all about it, give you the low down on the savings you can expect, and then present several of our favorite recipes to make from it. We only hope that you and your family enjoy these recipes as much as our families do.

SAVING MONEY!

It's about time! With our country at a crossroads over spending, there is no better time to start reaping the benefits of bulk shopping.

Restaurants have always been able to buy in bulk from their suppliers, but it wasn't until the 1970's, when Price Club opened its doors in San Diego, that buying in bulk became an option for the general public. In 1993 Price Club merged with Costco, and today they are the third largest retailer in the United States.

There are thousands of warehouse clubs nationwide, such as Costco, BJ's, and Sam's Club, that allow anyone who is willing to pay a small annual membership fee to have the buying power that restaurants have had for years. Because of the high demand for this money saving option, the major grocery chains and retailers like Super Wal-Mart began stocking their cases with bulk "family packs". Now everyone can buy in bulk at any one of these options found virtually

anywhere in the country, and save big money doing it. Now everyone can shave as much as 40% on their shopping bills.

But there is one big dilemma. The typical family cannot eat the amount of food that a restaurant serves in one day. They need to be able to extend the life of the foods they buy in bulk from a few days to a year in order to properly take advantage of the discounts. Saving money can quickly become wasting money if good food is left to spoil.

SAVING FOOD!

Since the advent of the FoodSaver® vacuum sealing system in 1986, this dilemma has been solved. The FoodSaver®, along with other commercial-quality home vacuum sealers, gives everyone the ability to vacuum pack their meats, fish, poultry, produce, soups, stews, stocks, dry goods, and more for storing in a home refrigerator, freezer, or pantry.

Since their introduction, home vacuum sealing appliances have helped millions of households just like yours to save money by buying in bulk. They quickly remove the enemy of fresh food—air—since removing the oxygen from vacuum sealing bags, jars, and canisters can significantly reduce the breakdown and spoiling of fresh food. Home vacuum sealers have even helped all but do away with the greatest enemy of bulk meat purchases—freezer burn! Ordinary, loose fitting, zipped, or tied freezer bags allow air to remain in the bag and moisture to escape onto the surface of the food; an unpleasant combination that produces freezer burn. Non-vacuum sealed foods can lose their color and taste due to unpleasant freezer burn after just a

few weeks in the freezer. Foods that are properly vacuum sealed will retain their flavor, color, and moisture for up to a year. This also means that hunters and fishermen can also seal and save their game and catches of the season for meals all through the year.

With its quality and reliability as a long-term and short-term storage method, there's no wonder why vacuum sealing is the standard for storing food in most restaurants and the rest of the commercial food industry. With affordable home vacuum sealing appliances now readily available, we recommend vacuum sealing become your standard for home repackaging of bulk purchased foods.

Be sure to read all of the instructions and tips included with your individual vacuum sealing appliance before use. These instructions will explain how to properly prepare your food for vacuum sealing with your particular appliance. Each machine has its own particular guidelines to ensure that your food is properly sealed for optimum freshness. That said, here are a few of our favorite vacuum sealing tips:

• Always dry whole pieces of meat or fish thoroughly with a paper towel before vacuum sealing.

• Hamburger, meatballs, and breaded foods should be frozen first on wax paper lined trays, and then vacuum sealed.

• Marinated foods and stews should be stored in a bag with at least three inches of unused space at the open end, so that there is proper room for the vacuum to be created.

• In combination with refrigeration, vacuum sealing also helps to inhibit the growth of mold, yeast, and bacteria. For instance, five-pound cheese blocks can be easily repackaged into smaller one-pound blocks, and mold growth

In a survey of 6,000 people, Costco was found to be the country's favorite mass grocer.

Source: Market Force Information Inc.
January 2010

will be eliminated since you only open what you need.

• For large amounts of food that you use small amounts of often, leave extra space at the end of the vacuum bag. This way, you can reseal after each use.

SAVING FOR LIFE!

Unless you are going to use all of a bulk meat or fish package right away, you are going to need to divide and vacuum seal your purchases for future use within a couple of days. How often you shop and how much you buy is only limited by the available room in your freezer(s) and the time you have to process your bulk food purchases. You don't have to start big.

Over time, as buying in bulk becomes a habit, you will start to build up an inventory of vacuum packed roasts, chops, steaks, fillets, stews, and other foods that are ready to cook or reheat at a moment's notice.

Our suggestion is that you read through the chapter introductions in the book and get a feel for what cuts of meat and fish you would like to cook in the next couple of weeks. If you are a first timer, start with just a couple of bulk packages. At the end of your first trip, and once the bulk packages are divided, you should have enough meat to prepare as many as 8 of the recipes in this book. As you start to get the hang of breaking down the large packages and preparing them for the refrigerator or freezer, you will discover that it is actually quite easy. Then you might want to tackle four or more packages.

What our families have done for years is plan a warehouse club trip twice a month. Before going, we decide the meats and fish we want to buy, select our recipes, and add to our shopping list any accompanying pantry or fresh ingredients we may need. This way, we are the most prepared for shopping, as warehouse clubs can often be an easy place to lose track of time!

Another great idea to ease you into bulk shopping is to shop with a close friend, splitting some of the costs and items between both families. This way, you can both go home with a better variety of items at the heavily reduced prices of buying in bulk. Return to either your or your friend's house and work together dividing and vacuum sealing any meats or perishable items.

Don't just take our word on the savings. One of the most rewarding things you can do is to calculate your savings for yourself. We recommend that you visit your regular grocery store and check the regular, small pack prices per pound, and jot them down next to your planned bulk purchases. Then, when you go bulk shopping, you will see immediately what you are saving per pound.

Once you get into the habit, you will be surprised at how quickly your savings can multiply. Some weeks, you will have enough cuts of meat in your freezer and ingredients in your pantry to skip grocery shopping all together! (Those are the best kinds of weeks!) Other weeks you will only need a few fresh vegetables or pantry items to complete your stockpiled meals. (Those weeks are still pretty good!)

When *you* see *your* very real savings, we promise you that buying in bulk will become a way of life for you and your family. It has for us and ours! Oh, and you may just become a better cook too!

PANTRY LIST

Bulk up on these items to easily prepare recipes from this book at only a moment's notice!

SPICES

granulated garlic

garlic powder

onion powder

cumin

cayenne pepper

chili powder

coriander

Italian seasoning

basil

rosemary

tarragon

oregano

thyme

bay leaves

red pepper flakes

parsley flakes

ground mustard

ground ginger

paprika

curry powder

cornstarch

DRY GOODS

beef broth

chicken broth

vegetable broth

minced garlic

canned diced tomatoes

Dijon mustard

all purpose flour

ketchup

sugar

light brown sugar

vegetable oil

olive oil

cider vinegar

Worcestershire sauce

soy sauce

powdered onion soup mix

marinara sauce

honey

barbecue sauce

salsa

hot sauce

PERISHABLES

bell peppers

carrots

celery

potatoes

mushrooms

parsnips

garlic

onions

scallions

lemons

butter

cream cheese

Parmesan cheese

sour cream

eggs

bacon

fresh herbs

TRI TIP STEAK

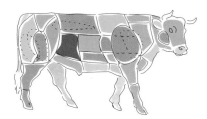

After a cow is slaughtered, it is cut into four pieces, or quarters, for easy handling. The best, or 'primal', cuts of beef are the chuck, brisket, shank, rib, short plate, short loin, sirloin, flank, and round. We begin our beef section with the tri tip, which is cut from the bottom sirloin primal cut. It has a pronounced grain that runs in a curve through its length. When slicing, you will want to follow the grain as it changes, and always cut against the grain for tenderness.

Also known as a round tip roast, tri tips are usually one of the lowest cost cuts of beef. When cooked properly, they are also one of the most delicious cuts of beef. Tri tips make very tender roasts that are great for barbecuing, especially when marinated before cooking. They also adapt well to the bold flavors of dry rubs. A trick to keeping this very lean cut of meat moist is to not trim any fat whatsoever until after cooking. What little fat is there, needs to stay on to tenderize (and flavor!) the meat as it cooks. Roasted tri tips and barbecued tips make the absolute best leftover roast beef sandwiches.

When a steak is cut from this roast it is called a tri tip steak. Whole round tips or tri tips are traditionally roasted, braised, or marinated and grilled. Round tip ends are perfect for stews.

Round or tri tips sold in bulk can vary greatly in size. The ones we like best are about 2 to 3 pounds, and can usually be purchased at a savings of around 40% when bought whole.

Vacuum sealed tri tips can usually be kept refrigerated for up to 10 days if purchased with a good 'sell by' date, or frozen for up to 1 year. If your tri tip is not vacuum sealed, you should divide and/or prepare it for storage within 2 or 3 days of purchase. Use a large chef's knife to divide the whole roast when you are going to use it for steaks and stews.

We give you one of Bob's slow cooker stroganoff recipes in this section, as we both agree that tri tip stroganoff is the best! Another great recipe in this section is Jan's more gourmet Stuffed Round Steak in Red Wine Sauce.

CONTENTS

Stuffed Round Steak in Red Wine Sauce

STUFFED ROUND STEAK IN RED WINE SAUCE

prep time **30** mins | cook time **1 ¾** hrs | serves **6-8** people | Jan Muller

This beautiful roast is stuffed with a vegetable stuffing mixture that is secretly only half-homemade. While it takes some prep-work to put this together, the presentation is most certainly worth it!

1. Preheat oven to 350 degrees.

2. Combine diced carrot, celery, onion, and cooked stuffing. Lay steak out flat and fill with the vegetable stuffing. Roll up and secure with twine. Generously season rolled steak with salt and pepper.

3. Add 2 tablespoons of the oil to an oven safe pan over high heat. Place rolled steak in the hot pan and rotate to brown on all sides. Remove from pan.

4. Add remaining 1 tablespoon of oil, quartered onions, celery lengths, and carrot lengths to the pan, and cook 5 minutes to brown. Add garlic, bay leaves, and thyme, and cook 2 minutes.

5. Add red wine and beef broth to the pan, and scrape the bottom of the pan to loosen bits. Bring to a boil and remove pan from heat.

SHOPPING LIST

3 pounds **round tip steak**, pounded out thin

1 carrot, finely diced

1 stalk **celery**, finely diced

½ medium **onion**, finely diced

1 box **stuffing**, cooked

salt and **pepper**

3 tablespoons **olive oil**

2 large onions, quartered

2 stalks **celery**, cut into **2** inch lengths

2 large carrots, cut into **2** inch lengths

2 cloves **garlic**, minced

3 bay leaves

2 tablespoons **fresh thyme**

1 cup **red wine**

6 cups **beef broth** or **stock**

6. Return rolled steak to pan, cover, and place in oven, baking 45 minutes. Flip the steak roll, re-cover, and bake an additional 45 minutes. Let rest 10 minutes before slicing. Serve with vegetables and juices from the pan.

HELPFUL TIPS

Use a meat mallet or rolling pin to flatten the steak out real well, ensure that it will be thin enough to roll up.

beef

MARINATED AND GRILLED TRI TIP STEAK

prep time **5** mins   cook time **12** mins   serves **8** people   Jan Muller

Grilled round or tri tip steaks can often be tough to chew, but this marinade makes the meat tender before it even hits the grill. While I suggest using fresh rosemary, you can use any fresh herbs you please.

SHOPPING LIST

8 (6-ounce) **tri tip steaks**

MARINADE

¼ cup **soy sauce**, regular or reduced sodium

¼ cup **olive oil**

2 cloves **garlic**, minced

1 ½ teaspoons minced **fresh rosemary**

¼ teaspoon **pepper**

1. Whisk together all marinade ingredients.

2. Seal steaks and marinade in a vacuum seal bag, and marinate in the refrigerator overnight.

3. Remove steaks from marinade and rest for 30 minutes.

4. Lightly oil or spray a grill or indoor grill pan, and then heat on high.

5. Place steaks on the hot grill and cook for 3-5 minutes on each side.

6. Transfer steak to a section of the grill with medium heat and continue to cook for an additional 2 minutes for medium rare doneness. Serve immediately.

HELPFUL TIPS

To make this steak even more tender, tenderize by repeatedly piercing with forks before sealing with the marinade in step 2.

TRI TIP STEAK SMOTHERED IN SWEET ONIONS

prep time **20** mins   cook time **1** hour   serves **4** people   Bob Warden

You can use any type of onion for this sweet onion smothered steak dish, but the Oso Sweet variety is almost certainly my favorite. They're even sweeter than Vidalia onions, which would be my second choice for this dish if Oso Sweet weren't available.

1. Add 1 tablespoon of the oil to a sauté pan over high heat.

2. Generously season steaks with salt and pepper, and then lightly sprinkle with flour.

3. Sear steaks in the hot pan until browned and then remove.

SHOPPING LIST

1 ½ pounds **tri tip steak**, cut into **4** steaks

2 tablespoons **olive oil**

salt and **pepper**

1 tablespoon **flour**

2 large sweet onions, sliced thinly

1 tablespoon **light brown sugar**

1 tablespoon **tomato paste**

1 tablespoon **fresh thyme**

1 pinch **red pepper flakes**

4. Add remaining tablespoon of oil to the sauté pan. Add onions and cook 5 minutes or until soft. Return meat to sauté pan.

5. Place 1 ¼ cups tap water in a mixing bowl and then whisk in all remaining ingredients. Pour mixture into pan, reduce heat to low, cover, and simmer for 1 hour.

6. Season sauce with salt and pepper to taste, and then serve steaks smothered in onions and sauce.

HELPFUL TIPS

To enhance the flavor of the dish, I sometimes switch out ¼ cup of the tap water in step 5 with ¼ cup of red wine.

Slow Cooked Beef Stroganoff

prep time **10** mins   cook time **8+** hrs   serves **6-8** people   Bob Warden

Beef Stroganoff doesn't get much simpler than this one. Packed with mushroom flavor from both canned mushroom soup and fresh mushrooms, the real trick to this recipe's success is cream cheese—it makes the final dish extra, extra creamy!

SHOPPING LIST

2 pounds **tri tip steak,** cubed

2 (**10.75**-ounce) cans **cream of mushroom soup**

14-16 ounces sliced **button mushrooms**

1 teaspoon **ground mustard**

2 tablespoons **Worcestershire sauce**

⅔ cup **beef broth** or **stock**

1 pound **cream cheese,** cubed

salt and **pepper**

1. Add the cream of mushroom soup, mushrooms, mustard, Worcestershire sauce, and beef broth to a slow cooker set on low.

2. Stir in steak cubes and cook 8-9 hours, or until steak is fork tender.

3. Add the cream cheese to the slow cooker, and stir until completely melted.

4. Add salt and pepper to taste before serving.

HELPFUL TIPS

Stroganoff is best served over hot buttered egg noodles with chopped parsley. Just don't forget to season your noodles with salt and pepper to ensure you don't end up with an under-seasoned final dish.

Beef Tenderloin

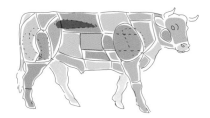

Most whole beef tenderloins sold in bulk average six pounds and can usually be purchased at a savings of 40%, when compared to the cost of individual filet mignon steaks. Vacuum sealed beef tenderloins can usually be kept refrigerated for up to 10 days if purchased with a good 'sell by' date, or frozen for up to 1 year. If your tenderloin is not vacuum sealed, you should divide and/ or prepare it for storage within 2 or 3 days of purchase. If you do not wish to leave it whole for roasting, use a large chef's knife to divide the tenderloin into steaks, tips, or a combination of the two. It should take you only a few minutes to prepare your tenderloin for refrigerating or long term freezing.

A whole beef tenderloin is usually around 3 to 4 inches in diameter at the big end, tapering down to less than an inch at the small end. Most tenderloins are about 18 inches long and can be left as 1 roast (Chateaubriand), cut into several filet mignon steaks, or cut into smaller tenderloin tips.

Beef Tenderloins, if not pre-trimmed, take a few minutes of work to remove the excess fat and silverskin. Beginning at the small end, slide a boning knife under the silverskin, and with two fingers and thumb of your free hand, gently slide the knife a couple of inches at a time along the underside of the skin, until you reach the opposite end. You may have to repeat this process if any layers of silverskin still remain.

When cutting steaks from the tenderloin, we recommend that you cut them to your desired thickness and then vacuum seal in packs of two or more.

Pieces of the small end of the tenderloin that are too small to be used for steaks can be cut into cubes for stew, or into strips for stir-fries, fajitas, or quesadillas.

The recipes in this section are for roasts and filet mignon steaks. They include Bob's favorite, individual Filet Mignon Wellingtons with Tarragon, which are cut from the smaller end of the whole tenderloin.

CONTENTS

Bacon Wrapped Filet Mignons

BACON WRAPPED FILET MIGNONS

prep time **15** mins   cook time **14** mins   serves **4** people   Jan Muller

Beef and bacon are a nice combination, as the slightly smoky flavor of the bacon brings out the sweetness of the beef. Bacon wrapped filet mignons like these are easily the most "classic" preparation of tenderloin filets. Assemble the bacon and steaks in advance, then vacuum seal and freeze in order to save prep time later. You can also extend the shelf life of your bacon by vacuum sealing any unused slices after opening.

SHOPPING LIST

4 (6-ounce) **beef tenderloin filets**

1 tablespoon **olive oil**

salt and **pepper**

¼ teaspoon **granulated garlic**

8 slices **bacon**

4 tablespoons minced **onion**

1. Place oven rack in its highest position and preheat broiler.

2. Rub steaks with olive oil and season generously with salt, pepper, and granulated garlic.

3. Criss-cross 2 slices of bacon around each steak and secure the loose ends together by inserting a toothpick into the bottom of the steak.

4. Place steaks on a broiler pan and broil for 5 to 7 minutes. Flip steaks, top each with 1 tablespoon of minced onion, and continue to broil for another 5 to 7 minutes for medium rare doneness.

5. Transfer steaks to plates and serve immediately.

HELPFUL TIPS

If you cook your bacon halfway before preparing, not only will the bacon be extra crispy, but then you can also substitute the rendered bacon fat for the olive oil in the recipe.

FILET MIGNON WITH GREEN PEPPERCORN SAUCE

prep time **15** mins　cook time **14** mins　serves **6-8** people　Jan Muller

Filet mignon is a beautiful, tender cut of meat that really begs for a luxurious sauce such as the Green Peppercorn one in this recipe. You may not know it, but green peppercorns are actually immature black peppercorns. They generally come packed in brine and have a slightly tangy flavor, which works well in the buttery, creamy sauce.

SHOPPING LIST

6 (6-ounce) **beef tenderloin filets**

1 tablespoon **olive oil**

salt and **pepper**

1 strip **bacon**, cooked and minced, grease reserved

2 tablespoons minced **onion**

¼ cup **mushrooms**, sliced

2 tablespoons **unsalted butter**

1 tablespoon **green peppercorns**, drained

2 tablespoons **bourbon**, optional

½ cup **beef broth**

¾ cup **heavy cream**

1. Place oven rack in its highest position and preheat broiler.

2. Rub steaks with olive oil and season generously with salt and pepper. Place steaks on broiler pan and place under broiler for 5 to 7 minutes. Flip steaks, and broil for another 5 to 7 minutes.

3. Meanwhile, heat a large sauté pan over high heat. Add reserved bacon grease and minced onions, and sauté until onions are soft.

4. Add mushrooms and 1 tablespoon of the butter to the pan, and sauté until soft. Add the green peppercorns, heat through, and pour off excess grease.

5. Add bourbon, minced bacon, beef broth, heavy cream, and remaining tablespoon of butter to the pan and bring to a simmer. Let the sauce reduce by simmering until slightly thickened. Add salt and pepper to taste.

6. Transfer finished steaks to plates, spoon sauce over top, and serve immediately.

HELPFUL TIPS

I suggest buying your mushrooms in bulk, and then slicing and cooking them all at once. After they have cooled down, vacuum seal and freeze them so that you have cooked mushrooms ready to go whenever you need them.

BEEF TENDERLOIN ROAST WITH CHO-CHO SAUCE

prep time **15** mins   cook time **45** mins   serves **6-8** people   Bob Warden

This ridiculously easy dish is the perfect meal for last minute guests. With just four ingredients, it leaves me to enjoy my company while it fills the house with a wonderful aroma. On the rare occasion that I have leftovers, I slice the roast, add a tablespoon of Cho-Cho sauce, roll it up in a tortilla shell, and microwave for a quick snack.

SHOPPING LIST

1 beef tenderloin roast, about **3** pounds

3 tablespoons **extra virgin olive oil**

¾ cup **soy sauce**, regular or reduced sodium

½ cup **hoisin sauce**

1. Preheat oven to 350 degrees.

2. Add 1 ½ tablespoons of the extra virgin olive oil to a large sauté pan over high heat.

3. In a bowl, whisk together remaining 1 ½ tablespoons of extra virgin olive oil with soy sauce and hoisin sauce to make the Cho-Cho sauce. Coat roast with ¼ cup of the prepared sauce.

4. In the hot sauté pan, sear all sides of the sauce-coated roast until nice and brown. Remove browned roast to a large baking dish. Add ½ cup sauce to sauté pan, whisking to heat evenly, before pouring over roast.

5. Bake roast uncovered for 45 minutes for medium rare doneness.

6. Remove roast from oven, transfer to a cutting board, and let stand 10 minutes. Combine hot juices at bottom of baking dish with remaining ½ cup of sauce. Slice roast and serve with the sauce on the side.

HELPFUL TIPS

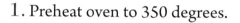

A bulk package of beef tenderloin gives you enough meat for two batches of this recipe. If you double the Cho-Cho sauce, you can coat the second roast with ¼ cup of sauce, vacuum seal it, and freeze so that you are ready for the next time you want to serve this dish. The remaining sauce will hold in your refrigerator for several weeks.

Filet Mignon Wellingtons with Tarragon

FILET MIGNON WELLINGTONS WITH TARRAGON

prep time **20** mins   cook time **35** mins   serves **6** people   Bob Warden

Traditionally, Beef Wellington is a whole beef tenderloin that is coated with liver pâté and a mushroom duxelle and wrapped in puffed pastry. I have turned them into individual portions and taken out the liver pâté, making it an easier dish that everyone will not only be impressed with, but also love.

SHOPPING LIST

6 (8-ounce) **beef filet mignon steaks**

¼ cup **unsalted butter**

1 pound **fresh mushrooms**, finely chopped

½ cup finely chopped **fresh onion**

¼ cup **dry sherry**

¼ cup finely chopped **fresh tarragon**

salt and **pepper**

1 (17.5-ounce) package **frozen puffed pastry sheets**, thawed

2 large eggs

1. Preheat oven to 425 degrees.

2. Heat butter in a sauté pan over medium heat until sizzling. Add the mushrooms, onion, sherry, and tarragon, and sauté until almost all of the liquid has evaporated. Generously season with salt and pepper, remove from pan, and divide into six equal portions.

3. Place one filet in the center of a puffed pastry sheet and top with one portion of mushroom mixture. Pull all edges of puffed pastry up over the top of the filet and crimp together. Place on a sheet pan and repeat for remaining five servings.

4. In a mixing bowl, whisk eggs with 2 tablespoons of tap water. Brush the mixture over top of the puffed pastry.

5. Place sheet pan of Beef Wellingtons in preheated oven and bake uncovered for 35 minutes for medium rare doneness.

6. Remove from oven and let rest 10 minutes. Can be served individually or cut in half and shared.

HELPFUL TIPS

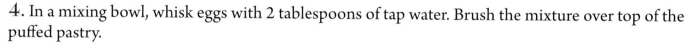

You can prepare the Beef Wellingtons ahead of time up to step 4, vacuum seal, and freeze. Then when you need them, remove from the vacuum seal bag, coat them with an egg wash, and bake for 45 minutes. The extra 10 minutes is necessary when cooking them from frozen.

Beef Tenderloin Steak with Rich Balsamic Glaze

prep time **15** mins   cook time **15** mins   serves **6-8** people   Jan Muller

Beef tenderloin is traditionally a more expensive cut of meat, but the wonderful melding of flavors in this dish makes it well worth the cost. Still, buying a whole beef tenderloin is a good way to save money. After you cut the steaks for this recipe, simply cube the remaining meat and then vacuum seal and freeze it for stews and soups.

Shopping List

6 (6-ounce) **beef tenderloin filets**

¾ cup **balsamic vinegar**

½ cup **cider vinegar**

¼ cup **light brown sugar**

1 tablespoon **olive oil**

salt and **pepper**

1. Heat a large sauté pan and a saucepan, both over high heat.

2. In a bowl, whisk together both vinegars and brown sugar. Add to hot saucepan and reduce until a thick, almost syrupy, consistency.

3. Rub oil onto steaks and season them with a generous amount of salt and pepper. Place steaks in hot sauté pan and cook for 3 to 5 minutes to brown. Flip the steaks and cook for another 3 to 5 minutes.

4. Pour balsamic glaze over steaks and cook for another 3 minutes. Flip the steaks again, baste with glaze from the pan, and cook another 2 minutes for medium rare doneness.

5. Transfer steaks to plates, spoon glaze over top, and serve immediately.

Helpful Tips

Brown sugar is an inexpensive way to turn vinegars into syrups. You can make a big batch of this syrup and have it as a house condiment, ready to serve with anything from beef to strawberries.

BRISKET

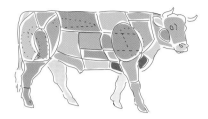

The brisket consists of the beef's breast, which also contains ribs and breastbone. What is commonly called a 'brisket' when it reaches the meat counter has (thankfully) had the ribs and breastbone removed. This boneless brisket is very tough and contains a lot of fat in the muscle. This makes brisket very well suited for moist-heat techniques, such as braising and simmering.

The brisket is chock full of flavor, but it just takes a good, slow cook to tenderize. Brisket is the cut usually used to make corned beef and pastrami.

Most briskets packaged for bulk purchase are the fattier triangle shaped portion of the meat, cut from the whole brisket. They weigh in at around 4 pounds. We recommend that you do not remove excess fat before cooking, as the meat needs as much as it can get to help keep itself moist during the long cooking process. Like flank steak, the brisket has a pronounced grain and porosity that takes well to flavored rubs and marinades. It especially goes well with sweet marinades that incorporate honey, barbecue sauce, ketchup, or beer. It is often a cut of choice for a slow smoked barbecue pit.

After cooking, always slice against the grain for easier chewing. Thin slices will also be more tender, and expose more flavors with each bite.

Vacuum sealed brisket can usually be kept refrigerated for up to 10 days if purchased with a good 'sell by' date, or frozen for up to 1 year. If your brisket is not vacuum sealed, you should divide and/or prepare it for storage within 2 or 3 days of purchase.

CONTENTS

Honey Barbecued Beef Brisket

HONEY BARBECUED BEEF BRISKET

prep time **35** mins   cook time **6-7** hrs   serves **8** people   Jan Muller

Liquid smoke, as implied by its name, is used in this recipe to add a nice smoky flavor without having to light a grill. I have no idea how they make liquid smoke, but it is pretty incredible stuff.

1. Combine onion powder and garlic with the first measure of liquid smoke and coat the brisket with the mixture. Vacuum seal and marinate up to 24 hours.

2. Preheat oven to 300 degrees.

3. Remove brisket from vacuum seal, place in baking dish, cover, and cook for 5 to 6 hours.

4. In a saucepan, combine brown sugar, beef broth, ketchup, butter, the second measure of liquid smoke, ground mustard, and honey. Add salt and pepper to taste and then heat until bubbly hot.

5. Meanwhile, remove the brisket from the oven, slice, and return to baking dish.

6. Pour the hot sauce over the sliced brisket, add carrots and onions, cover, and return to the oven for 1 additional hour.

SHOPPING LIST

1 beef brisket, about **4** pounds

1 tablespoon **onion powder**

1 tablespoon **granulated garlic**

2 tablespoons **liquid smoke**

1 ½ tablespoons **light brown sugar**

¼ cup **beef broth**

1 cup **ketchup**

3 tablespoons **butter**

1 tablespoon **liquid smoke**

1 ½ teaspoons **ground mustard**

2 tablespoons **honey**

salt and **pepper**

4 carrots, cut into **1** inch pieces

2 large red onions, cut into sixths

HELPFUL TIPS

The flavor of liquid smoke is very intense. You might want to play it safe the first time you try this recipe and skip the second measure of liquid smoke that is added to the barbecue sauce.

Salsa-fied Barbecued Beef Brisket

beef

prep time **10** mins cook time **6-7** hrs serves **8** people Bob Warden

Marinating a brisket in salsa may sound strange, but the acid from the tomato helps to slightly break down the meat for more tenderness. I like to use a real spicy salsa and a chipotle flavored barbecue sauce, but I'll leave that decision up to you!

Shopping List

1 **beef brisket**, about 4 pounds

1 cup **salsa**

1 teaspoon **granulated garlic**

1 cup **barbecue sauce**

salt and **pepper**

1. Combine the salsa and granulated garlic. Coat the brisket with the mixture, vacuum seal, and marinate for up to 24 hours.

2. Preheat oven to 300 degrees.

3. Remove brisket from vacuum seal and scrape and reserve the salsa. Place brisket in a baking dish, cover, and cook for 5 to 6 hours.

4. Pour reserved salsa and barbecue sauce into a saucepan over high heat and bring to a boil. Boil for 5 minutes. Season the sauce with salt and pepper to taste.

5. Remove the baked brisket from the oven, slice, and return to the baking dish.

6. Pour the boiled sauce over the sliced brisket, cover, and return to the oven for 1 additional hour before serving.

Helpful Tips

Boiling the sauce in step 4 is not entirely necessary, as long as you make sure to bake it with the brisket for 1 hour to thoroughly heat the salsa that was marinating with the raw meat. Just add a small pinch of salt and pepper, rather than adding it to taste.

SPICY FRENCH ONION BRISKET

prep time **5** mins   cook time **8-10** hrs   serves **8-10** people   Bob Warden

This brisket is great served alongside your favorite sides, especially mashed potatoes, but I also really enjoy it as a sandwich in a chewy roll with a slice of Swiss cheese. Keep in mind that dried soup mixes have salt in them already, so there is no need to add any more to this dish.

SHOPPING LIST

1 beef brisket, about **4 pounds**

1 (**1**-ounce) packet **powdered onion soup mix**

1 teaspoon **granulated garlic**

1 (**12**-ounce) bottle **chili sauce**

1 ½ cups **beef broth** or **stock**

pepper

1. Coat the brisket with the onion soup mix and granulated garlic, vacuum seal, and marinate for up to 24 hours.

2. Remove brisket and place in a slow cooker.

3. Whisk together the chili sauce and beef broth, pour over brisket, cover the slow cooker, and let cook for 8 to 10 hours on low heat. Season with pepper to taste.

4. Slice the brisket and serve with sauce poured over top.

HELPFUL TIPS

I often slice an onion and add it in with the rest of the ingredients to the slow cooker, as a nice sweet onion adds to the spice of the chili sauce.

FLANK STEAK

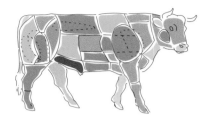

Flank Steak, also known as London Broil, is a single muscle that comes from beneath the loin and in front of the back legs. It is generally about 1 inch thick at one end and up to 2 inches thick at the other, more flat end. They can weigh from as little as 1 pound to as much as 3 ½ pounds. The muscle grain in this cut of meat is quite coarse and runs lengthwise from end to end. Flank steak has very little fat and almost no connective tissue. Because it is also quite porous, it soaks up marinades extremely well for extremely flavorful results. If freezing, adding the marinade to the vacuum sealed bag beforehand will ensure that it will be ready to go whenever you need it. As it is a fairly thin cut of meat, thawing time is quite quick.

Vacuum sealed flank steaks can usually be kept refrigerated for up to 10 days if purchased with a good 'sell by' date, or frozen for up to 1 year. If your flank steak is not vacuum sealed, you should divide and/or prepare it for storage within 2 or 3 days of purchase.

Some flank steaks come with a bit of tough silverskin attached to the top surface. You will want to remove this before cooking. Beginning at the small end, slide a boning knife under the silverskin, and with two fingers and thumb of your free hand, gently slide the knife a couple of inches at a time along the underside of the skin, until you reach the opposite end. You may have to repeat this process if any layers of silverskin still remain.

To help keep flank steak from curling up when exposed to the high heat of grilling or broiling make shallow crisscross cuts on both sides of the steak about half of an inch apart.

When removing flank steak from a hot grill or broiler, it is important to let the steak rest for about 10 minutes before slicing. This will allow the juices to redistribute evenly throughout the steak, rather than escaping at first slice. Always cut against the grain when slicing for easy chewing. Thin slices will be more tender.

CONTENTS

GRILLED GINGER AND MUSTARD FLANK STEAK

prep time **5** mins — cook time **20** mins — serves **6** people — Jan Muller

There is nothing like grilled steak any time of the year. I first used a combination of ground ginger and mustard on turkey breast, but one day I thought to try it on flank steak, and I am glad I did!

SHOPPING LIST

1 ½ pound **flank steak**, trimmed

1 ½ tablespoons **olive oil**

2 tablespoons **ground mustard**

2 tablespoons **ground ginger**

salt and **pepper**

1. Heat a grill or indoor grill pan on high.

2. Coat steak with olive oil.

3. Rub mustard and ginger into steak, and then generously season with salt and pepper.

4. Place steak on the hottest part of the grill for 3 to 4 minutes on each side.

5. Transfer steak to a section of the grill with medium heat, close the lid, and continue to cook for an additional 10 minutes for medium rare doneness. Let rest 10 minutes before slicing thin to serve.

HELPFUL TIPS

Using a meat tenderizer before grilling or searing flank steak will help prevent it from curling up on you as it cooks.

Beef Fajitas the Slow Cooker Way

BEEF FAJITAS THE SLOW COOKER WAY

prep time **20** mins | cook time **8+** hrs | serves **6** people | Bob Warden

SHOPPING LIST

1 ½ pound **flank steak**, trimmed, cut into three pieces

1 ½ tablespoons **vegetable oil**

1 teaspoon **chili powder**

1 teaspoon **cumin**

1 teaspoon **ground coriander**

1 teaspoon **dry oregano**

1 large onion, thinly sliced

2 large red bell peppers, thinly sliced

2 cups **salsa**

salt and **pepper**

flour tortillas

I love to come home to a meal that's ready to eat, so I started using my slow cooker for recipes that traditionally you would never think to prepare in one. This recipe results in a most flavorful filling for fajitas that you can be eating within minutes of returning home from a long day at work.

1. Add oil to a sauté pan over high heat.

2. Combine chili powder, cumin, coriander, and oregano. Rub steak with the mixture.

3. Sear steaks in the hot pan until browned, and then transfer to a slow cooker.

4. Add onion and peppers to slow cooker, top with salsa, cover, and cook on low for 8-9 hours.

5. Remove steaks from the slow cooker, shred, and return shredded steak to cooker. Stir until steak is mixed back in with the other ingredients. Season to taste with salt and pepper.

6. To serve, wrap fajita mixture in warmed flour tortillas, topped with your favorite toppings such as shredded cheese, sour cream, or guacamole.

HELPFUL TIPS

Once I have rubbed the dry spice mixture onto the flank steak, I like to vacuum seal it and let it marinate overnight in the refrigerator to add more intensity to the flavors.

Pepper Steak

PEPPER STEAK

prep time **20** mins   cook time **30** mins   serves **6** people   Jan Muller   beef

SHOPPING LIST

1 ½ pound **flank steak**, trimmed, cut into strips

3 tablespoons **vegetable oil**

1 large onion, thickly sliced

3 large green bell peppers, thickly sliced

2 cups **canned diced tomatoes**, with juice

1 tablespoon **soy sauce**, regular or reduced sodium

1 ½ teaspoons **cornstarch**

salt and **pepper**

Pepper steak is an Asian classic that is actually easier to make at home than you would think. Pork or chicken can be substituted for a change of pace, but it doesn't get much better than flank steak and peppers! Serve alongside steamed rice or cooked linguine that has been quickly stir-fried in soy sauce and sesame oil.

1. Add 1 ½ tablespoons of the oil to a sauté pan over high heat.

2. Sear sliced steak in pan until browned. Remove from pan and reserve.

3. Add remaining 1 ½ tablespoons of oil, onion, and peppers to the pan and sauté until soft.

4. Return steak to pan, reduce heat to medium, and stir in diced tomatoes. Cover pan and simmer 5 minutes.

5. In a bowl, whisk ¼ cup of tap water into the soy sauce and cornstarch. Add mixture to the sauté pan and simmer until sauce is thick and clear. Season with salt and pepper to taste and serve immediately.

HELPFUL TIPS

For a better presentation, add a teaspoon of grated fresh ginger while cooking the onions and peppers, use three different colors of bell pepper to pop the color, and garnish with sliced scallions before serving.

TERIYAKI AND HONEY MARINATED FLANK STEAK

prep time **15** mins · cook time **20** mins · serves **6** people · Bob Warden

SHOPPING LIST

1 ½ pound **flank steak**, trimmed

2 tablespoons **cider vinegar**

2 tablespoons **light brown sugar**

1 ½ tablespoons **vegetable oil**

2 cloves **garlic**, minced

¼ teaspoon **pepper**

⅓ cup **teriyaki sauce**

2 tablespoons **honey**

Marinades, like the one used to marinate flank steak in this recipe, not only add a lot of flavor, but also tenderize the meat at the same time. Many bottled or homemade marinades also make great dipping sauces if you don't have the time to marinate the meat in them. Simply grill the meat with salt and pepper and then dip away!

1. Whisk the vinegar and brown sugar until sugar is dissolved, and then whisk in the remaining ingredients, except steak, to create a marinade.

2. Vacuum seal the steak in the marinade and refrigerate for at least 2 hours.

3. Lightly oil or spray a grill or indoor grill pan, and then heat on high.

4. Remove steak from marinade, and place on the hottest part of the grill for 3 to 4 minutes on each side. Watch out for flare ups when placing and turning steak.

5. Transfer steak to a section of the grill with medium heat, close the lid, and continue to cook for an additional 10 minutes for medium rare doneness. Let rest for 10 minutes before thinly slicing to serve.

HELPFUL TIPS

You can use the used marinade as a dipping sauce as long as you boil it for at least 5 minutes beforehand, as it was in contact with the raw meat.

GROUND BEEF

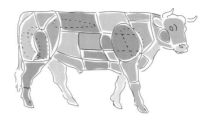

Our experience is that by buying in bulk from a warehouse club, or in family packs from your favorite grocer, you can save about 30% on your ground beef purchases.

However, not all ground beef is created equal. How much fat or water is left in the final product make a huge difference in the shrinkage, taste, and flavor of cooked ground beef. The percentage of fat content is listed right on the front of the label, and most people agree that the best tasting ground beef for hamburgers contains around 25% fat. We agree as well! However, many diets call for much leaner ground beef. Fortunately, you have a choice.

What is not on the front of the label is how much water may have been intentionally or inadvertently added to the ground beef during processing. The more water, the more you are paying for water and the less ground beef you are actually getting. Besides paying ground beef prices for water, this is also bad because you get a product that is difficult to properly brown, as the water cooks out and literally boils your ground beef. Our advice? Ask your butcher if they grind the hamburger frozen or refrigerated. When ground beef is ground from frozen beef, ice crystals are ground into the meat and add to the water content.

We like to vacuum seal homemade hamburgers from 2-4 burgers per vacuum pack, and freeze. You can even follow entire recipes for meatloaves or meatballs, prepping and forming them without cooking, and then vacuum seal for dinner on another night without any of the prep work! We even put the meatloaves right into loaf pans, vacuum sealing over the entire pan.

CONTENTS

Make That a Cheeseburger Pizza

MAKE THAT A CHEESEBURGER PIZZA

prep time **15** mins   cook time **30** mins   serves **4** people   Bob Warden

Whether this is a pizza or one giant open-faced cheeseburger is a question that I simply cannot answer. I can say that this recipe is a whole lot of fun for the family and may just disappear off the table in seconds. Serve alongside French fries!

1. Preheat oven to 425 degrees. Add olive oil to a sauté pan over high heat.

2. Add ground beef, salt, and pepper to hot pan and brown, approximately 10 minutes. Drain well.

3. Spread ketchup over pizza crust, sprinkle with garlic, shredded mozzarella, and cooked ground beef.

4. Arrange onion, tomatoes, and pickles over top beef.

SHOPPING LIST

1 pound **ground beef**

2 tablespoons **olive oil**

½ teaspoon **salt**

⅛ teaspoon **pepper**

½ cup **ketchup**

1 (**12**-inch) **prepared pizza crust**

¼ teaspoon **granulated garlic**

2 cups shredded **mozzarella cheese**

1 onion, sliced thin

2 tomatoes, sliced thin

15 slices **dill pickle**

¾ cup shredded **Cheddar cheese**

5. Top with cheddar cheese and bake 15-20 minutes, or until cheese is bubbly. Slice and serve.

HELPFUL TIPS

Prebaked crusts such as DiGiorno brand work best for this recipe as canned pizza crusts are too soft to hold up to the weight of all those ingredients!

ground beef

Chili Con Carne with Jalapeño Cornbread

prep time **40** mins   cook time **40** mins   serves **10+** people   Jan Muller

We all know that chili gets better with time, but this one is great right from the beginning. I highly recommend serving this dish as written: alongside a spicy and simple to prepare cornbread.

1. Heat bacon in a large stockpot over high heat. Cook until crispy, remove, and reserve.

2. Add ground beef to the hot pot of bacon grease, cook to brown, and then pour off excess grease.

3. Add red wine to the ground beef and simmer, until the liquid has reduced by half. Then add onions, garlic, carrots, celery, bell peppers, chili powder, cumin, oregano, thyme, paprika, red pepper flakes, and brown sugar. Cook until onions have softened.

4. Add tomato sauce and beef broth, bring to a simmer, and cook for 20 minutes.

5. Add kidney beans and reserved bacon, bring back up to a simmer, and then season with salt and pepper to taste.

6. Meanwhile, prepare the cornbread by following directions on the packages, adding jalapeños to the mixture before baking. Serve hot alongside chili, topped with Cheddar cheese.

Shopping List

3 pounds **ground beef**
4 slices **bacon**
½ cup **red wine**
2 **onions**, diced
3 cloves **garlic**, minced
2 **carrots**, diced
3 stalks **celery**, diced
2 **green bell peppers**, diced
2 tablespoons **chili powder**
1 teaspoon **cumin**
2 teaspoons **dry oregano**
1 teaspoon **dry thyme**
1 tablespoon **paprika**
1 tablespoon **red pepper flakes**
1 tablespoon **light brown sugar**
2 cups **tomato sauce**
1 cup **beef broth** or **stock**
1 (15-ounce) can **kidney beans**, drained
salt and **pepper**
2 boxes **cornbread mix**
2 **jalapeño peppers**, minced
1 cup shredded **Cheddar cheese**

Helpful Tips

If you don't like your cornbread spicy, do not add the jalapeño and try using a can of creamed corn instead, just reduce the liquid the package tells you to add by ½ cup.

LET'S CALL THEM SWEDISH MEATBALLS

prep time **15** mins   cook time **1** hour   serves **4** people   Bob Warden

This is definitely not the traditional preparation of Swedish Meatballs, but this personal creation with a Cheddar and mushroom sauce does remind me of that classic dish! Serve alongside mashed potatoes or over buttered egg noodles.

SHOPPING LIST

1 pound **ground beef**

nonstick cooking spray

1 large egg

¼ cup **breadcrumbs**

¼ cup minced **onion**

2 teaspoons minced **fresh tarragon**

1 (10.75-ounce) can **cream of Cheddar soup**

1 (10.75-ounce) can **cream of mushroom soup**

1 (12-ounce) can **evaporated milk**

salt and **pepper**

1. Preheat oven to 350 degrees. Spray a sheet pan with nonstick cooking spray.

2. Mix together ground beef, egg, breadcrumbs, onion, and 1 teaspoon of the tarragon. Form into 1 inch balls and place on greased sheet pan. Bake for 20 minutes.

3. Meanwhile, whisk together the cream of Cheddar soup, cream of mushroom soup, and evaporated milk to create the sauce. Add salt and pepper to taste.

4. Transfer baked meatballs to a plate of paper towels to drain excess grease and then transfer to a baking dish. Pour sauce over meatballs, cover dish with aluminum foil, and bake 30 minutes.

5. Uncover baking dish and bake an additional 10 minutes. Sprinkle with remaining tarragon and serve.

HELPFUL TIPS

Cook the meatballs ahead of time, vacuum seal, and freeze. Then when you need a last minute meal, just use the frozen meatballs, starting with step 3, and add 10-15 minutes to the baking time in step 4.

Bubblin' Brown Sugar Meatloaf

BUBBLIN' BROWN SUGAR MEATLOAF

prep time **20** mins — cook time **80** mins — serves **8** people — Bob Warden

The proof is not in the pudding, but in the brown sugar mixture that resides in and around this special meat loaf. My guests always ask for this recipe after I serve it.

SHOPPING LIST

2 pounds **ground beef**

½ packed cup **light brown sugar**

½ cup **ketchup**

1 tablespoon **cider vinegar**

2 large eggs

½ cup **milk**

1 onion, diced

¼ teaspoon **dry tarragon**

¾ cup **breadcrumbs**

¾ teaspoon **salt**

¼ teaspoon **pepper**

1. Preheat oven to 350 degrees.

2. Mix together brown sugar, ¼ cup of the ketchup, and vinegar. Spread mixture across the bottom of a 5x9 inch loaf pan.

3. Mix ground beef with remaining ingredients, including the other ¼ cup ketchup.

4. Pack meatloaf on top of brown sugar mixture in loaf pan.

5. Place loaf pan on a sheet pan, place in oven, and bake for 1 hour 20 minutes.

6. Let rest 15 minutes. Remove from pan, slice, and serve topped with drippings from the pan.

HELPFUL TIPS

You can also make this the traditional way, topping the loaf with the brown sugar mixture rather than cooking it at the bottom of the pan. Simply, drain juices from the loaf and top with the sauce halfway through cooking.

Spaghetti Sauce with Meatballs

SPAGHETTI SAUCE WITH MEATBALLS

prep time **20** mins · cook time **2+** hrs · serves **6** people · Bob Warden

I hear there are such things as ordinary meatballs, but these certainly aren't them! Simmered in a simple, homemade spaghetti sauce, you may just want to make a double batch of this one!

1. Heat a saucepot over high heat and add the ¼ cup olive oil, onion, garlic, carrot, bell pepper, and celery, sautéing until soft.

2. Add all remaining sauce ingredients to the saucepot, reduce heat to low, and simmer for 1 ½ hours.

3. Meanwhile, add the 2 tablespoons of olive oil to a sauté pan over high heat. Combine all other meatball ingredients and form into 12 meatballs. Place in the hot pan and brown on all sides. Remove to paper towels to drain excess grease.

4. Add meatballs to the sauce and simmer for an additional 30 minutes. Season with salt and pepper to taste before serving.

SHOPPING LIST

SPAGHETTI SAUCE
¼ cup **olive oil**
1 **onion**, diced
5 cloves **garlic**, minced
1 **carrot**, diced
1 **green bell pepper**, diced
1 stalk **celery**, diced
2 (28-ounce) cans **diced tomatoes**, with juice
1 teaspoon **sugar**
1 **bay leaf**
¾ teaspoon **Italian seasoning**

MEATBALLS
1 pound **ground beef**
2 tablespoons **olive oil**
1 cup **Italian breadcrumbs**
½ cup shredded **Parmesan cheese**
1 teaspoon **parsley flakes**
1 teaspoon **dry basil**
½ teaspoon **dry oregano**
⅛ teaspoon **granulated garlic**
2 **large eggs**
½ teaspoon **salt**
¼ teaspoon **pepper**

HELPFUL TIPS

Making a double batch and vacuum sealing and freezing half for a second meal can actually make these even better as the meatballs will have all the time in the world to absorb the delicious sauce.

FAST FOOD CASSEROLE

prep time **20** mins   cook time **55** mins   serves **8** people   Bob Warden

The cheese, bacon, and scallion topping in this dish highlights an already tasty mushroom and cheddar casserole. Of course, what really sets things apart is what is in the middle... French fries!

1. Preheat oven to 375 degrees. Heat a large sauté pan over high heat.

2. Add ground beef and onion to the pan and sauté until browned, approximately 10 minutes. Drain off excess grease.

3. Add garlic and both soups to the ground beef, heating thoroughly.

SHOPPING LIST

2 pounds **ground beef**

½ **onion**, diced

1 teaspoon **granulated garlic**

1 (**10.75**-ounce) can **cream of mushroom soup**

1 (**10.75**-ounce) can **cream of Cheddar soup**

1 (**26**-ounce) bag **frozen shoestring French fries**

2 cups shredded **Cheddar cheese**

12 slices **bacon**, cooked and crumbled

4 **scallions**, thinly sliced

4. Pour mixture into a 9x13 baking dish, top with fries and bake 25 to 30 minutes.

5. Top with Cheddar cheese, bacon, and scallions. Return to oven and bake for an additional 5-7 minutes, or until cheese is melted. Let rest 5-10 minutes before slicing.

HELPFUL TIPS

For extra crispy French fries in this casserole, simply pre-bake them according to the package directions before assembling. With cooked fries and a nice and hot ground beef mixture, you can skip the first 30 minutes of baking and only bake until the cheese is melted.

SLOPPY JANS

prep time **10** mins   cook time **40** mins   serves **6** people   Jan Muller

My twist on a classic, these Sloppy Jans are made special with salsa (yes salsa), Dijon mustard, and brown sugar. Personally, I like mine spicy, so I use the hottest salsa I can find.

1. Heat a large sauté pan over high heat.

2. Add ground beef, onion, green pepper, and garlic to the hot pan. Sauté to brown, approximately 10 minutes, and drain off excess grease.

3. In a mixing bowl, whisk together mustard, salsa, and brown sugar. Add mixture to the browned beef, reduce heat to low, and simmer for 30 minutes. Add salt and pepper to taste.

4. Serve immediately in split Kaiser rolls.

SHOPPING LIST

1 pound **ground beef**

¼ cup diced **onion**

¼ cup diced **green bell pepper**

1 teaspoon **minced garlic**

1 teaspoon **Dijon mustard**

¾ cup **salsa**

1 tablespoon **light brown sugar**

salt and **pepper**

6 Kaiser rolls

HELPFUL TIPS

For a more traditional taste, the salsa can be easily substituted with canned diced tomatoes.

Bacon and Onion Cheeseburger Sliders

BACON AND ONION CHEESEBURGER SLIDERS

prep time **10** mins · cook time **12** mins · serves **4** people · Jan Muller

With cheese in and on top of the burger patties, these are no ordinary sliders. The bacon is optional, but who would want to leave that out? Though this recipe is for 12 sliders, you can also make 6 double cheeseburger sliders for an even higher ratio of meat to bun (which is always better)!

SHOPPING LIST

1 pound **ground beef**

2 tablespoons **olive oil**

½ cup **ketchup**

½ cup shredded **Mexican cheese blend**

1 large egg

1 pinch **granulated garlic**

½ teaspoon **salt**

⅛ teaspoon **pepper**

¼ cup shredded **Cheddar cheese**

12 slider rolls

12 slices **bacon**, cut in half

iceberg lettuce

12 slices **plum tomato**

1 **onion**, sliced thinly

1. Add oil to a large sauté pan over high heat.

2. Mix beef, ketchup, Mexican cheese, egg, garlic, and salt, and pepper. Divide mixture into 12 meatballs and flatten to form burgers.

3. Add burgers to the hot pan and cook 3 to 5 minutes on each side. Top with Cheddar cheese and heat to melt.

4. Remove burgers from pan, place in buns, and top with bacon, lettuce, tomato, and onion. Serve immediately.

HELPFUL TIPS

Using two different types of cheeses isn't entirely necessary; you can purchase one bag of shredded cheese and use it for the filling and topping to save on the grocery bill.

Penne Bake

PENNE BAKE

prep time **20** mins   cook time **65** mins   serves **8+** people   Jan Muller

Similar to baked ziti, this dish is a lot like lasagna, only not nearly as labor intensive as arranging each individual layer by hand. In fact, I prefer the tubular shape of penne pasta to the flat lasagna noodles anyway!

1. Preheat oven to 350 degrees. Heat a large sauté pan over high heat.

2. Add beef, onion, and garlic to the hot pan and sauté until beef is browned, approximately 10 minutes. Pour off excess grease.

3. Add marinara sauce, basil, oregano, parsley, and chicken broth to the pan. Reduce heat to low and simmer for 15 minutes.

4. In a mixing bowl, stir cream cheese into the hot penne pasta, and then add 1 cup of the meat sauce, 1 ½ cups of the mozzarella, and ½ cup of the Parmesan, stirring well.

5. Pour penne mixture into a 9x13 baking dish and pour remaining sauce over top. Cover with aluminum foil and bake 30 minutes.

SHOPPING LIST

1 pound **ground beef**

1 cup diced **onion**

2 cloves **garlic**, minced

1 (**32**-ounce) jar **marinara sauce**

¼ teaspoon **dry basil**

¼ teaspoon **dry oregano**

½ teaspoon **dry parsley**

1 cup **chicken broth** or **stock**

8 ounces **cream cheese**, softened

1 pound **penne pasta**, cooked and drained

2 cups shredded **mozzarella cheese**

1 cup grated **Parmesan cheese**

6. Uncover and top with remaining ½ cup mozzarella cheese and ½ cup of Parmesan cheese. Return to oven and bake for an additional 10 minutes, or until cheese is melted. Let rest 10 minutes before slicing.

HELPFUL TIPS

8 ounces of ricotta cheese can be used in place of the cream cheese for an even more lasagna-style texture.

Lovin' It Lasagna

prep time **30** mins   cook time **1¼** hrs   serves **12** people   Jan Muller

I'm lovin' this lasagna thanks to the great combination of both ground beef and Italian sausage. You may want to make two though, because based on my experience, you may find that guests will be begging to take a slice home.

1. Preheat oven to 375 degrees. Heat a sauté pan over high heat.

2. Add beef, sausage, salt, and pepper to the hot pan and thoroughly brown (you may have to do this in batches). Drain and remove from pan.

3. Add onion and garlic to the hot pan, sauté until soft, and then combine with browned meat and marinara sauce.

4. In a mixing bowl, whisk together ricotta cheese and egg.

5. Layer prepared ingredients in a 9x13 dish starting with ⅓ of the meat sauce, followed by ⅓ of the Parmesan cheese, ⅓ of the pasta, ⅓ of the ricotta, and ⅓ of the mozzarella cheese. Repeat with two more layers of the same.

6. Cover with foil and bake 40 minutes. Uncover and bake an additional 20 minutes. Let rest 15 minutes before slicing.

Shopping List

1 pound **ground beef**

1 pound **Italian sausage**, removed from casing

½ teaspoon **salt**

¼ teaspoon **pepper**

½ cup minced **onion**

2 cloves **garlic**, crushed

1 (**32**-ounce) jar **marinara sauce**

16 ounces **ricotta cheese**

1 large **egg**

12 **lasagna noodles**

¾ cup grated **Parmesan cheese**

12 ounces sliced **mozzarella cheese**

Helpful Tips

You can use either sweet Italian or hot Italian sausage in the meat sauce, but I actually like to use a combination of ½ pound of each.

GROUND BEEF PATTIES

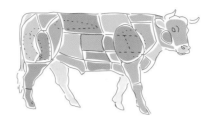

Amazingly, 100% ground beef patties are usually priced the same as bulk ground beef in most warehouse clubs. Our experience is that by buying in bulk from a warehouse club, or in family packs from your favorite grocer, you can save about 30% on your ground beef purchases.

The bad thing about pre-formed ground beef patties is that most packages offer very little protection from freezer burn. Usually packaged in nothing more than a bag inside of a cardboard box, as soon as you open that bag to remove a few patties for a family lunch, it's all downhill for the remaining patties.

Thankfully, repackaging bulk amounts of frozen ground beef patties is one of the easiest things you can do with a vacuum sealer. As the patties are already formed, frozen, and (usually) separated by wax paper, they can easily be transferred right into a vacuum sealing bag in seconds. Just be sure to leave plenty of extra room at the top of the bag to re-seal after those occasions that you only remove a few patties from the bag. You may also choose to vacuum seal them into smaller amounts of 4-8 patties per bag, so that you always have just the right amount for your family, whenever you need it.

In this category you will find that an ordinary burger patty need not stay ordinary! Bob's Hamburger Steak with Caramelized Onion and Mushroom Gravy makes a delicious fork and knife meal out of burger patties that definitely won't leave you missing the bun. And Jan's New Mexico Burger takes burgers (nearly) south of the border for a surprising cross between a burger and a burrito!

CONTENTS

HAMBURGER STEAK WITH CARAMELIZED ONIONS AND MUSHROOM GRAVY

beef

prep time **10** mins   cook time **45** mins   serves **6** people   Bob Warden

The caramelized onions and mushroom gravy in this recipe makes for the perfect antidote to the often-ordinary hamburger steak. Of course, for me anything with caramelized onions is a winner!

1. Add oil to a large sauté pan over high heat.

2. Place burgers in the hot pan, cook 6 to 8 minutes, flip, and cook for another 6 to 8 minutes. Remove from pan and reserve.

3. Add onions and mushrooms to the hot pan, cooking 12 to 15 minutes or until nice and caramelized.

SHOPPING LIST

6 (8-ounce) **hamburger patties**

2 tablespoons **olive oil**

1 cup thinly sliced **onions**

1 cup thinly sliced **mushrooms**

¼ cup **red wine**

¼ cup **all purpose flour**

2 cups **beef broth or stock**

salt and **pepper**

4. Add red wine to the pan and reduce until almost dry.

5. Sprinkle flour over onions and mushrooms and stir well, making sure to scrape the bottom of the pan to get bits.

6. Gradually whisk in beef broth. Continue whisking while simmering until gravy thickens.

7. Reduce heat to low, return burgers to pan, cover, and cook for about 15 minutes. Add salt and pepper to taste and serve immediately.

HELPFUL TIPS

For an extra rich gravy, melt 2 tablespoons of butter into the gravy right before serving.

Bacon Wrapped Burgers with Tomato Parmesan Dressing

prep time **10** mins   cook time **18** mins   serves **6** people   Jan Muller

beef

I've never met a naked burger that I liked, and this bacon wrapped and dressing smothered combination is the perfect example why. Sometimes less is definitely not more; when it comes to bacon, more is more!

1. Lightly oil or spray a grill or indoor grill pan, and then heat on high.

2. Wrap each burger with 2 bacon slices in a criss—cross fashion, secure with a toothpick, and place burgers on grill.

3. Grill 6 to 8 minutes, flip, and grill for another 6 to 8 minutes for medium, depending on your grill.

4. Place 2 slices of Cheddar cheese on each burger and heat to melt.

Shopping List

6 (8-ounce) **hamburger patties**

vegetable oil

12 slices **bacon**

12 slices **Cheddar cheese**

¼ cup **mayonnaise**

¼ cup **ketchup**

1 tablespoon **Worcestershire sauce**

1 tablespoon minced **onion**

1 tablespoon grated **Parmesan cheese**

6 hamburger buns

red leaf lettuce

5. Meanwhile, whisk together the mayonnaise, ketchup, Worcestershire sauce, onion, and Parmesan cheese to make the dressing.

6. Remove burgers from grill, place in buns, and top each with 1 ½ tablespoons of dressing and 2 lettuce leaves. Serve immediately.

Helpful Tips

Smoked gouda (or even smoked provolone) cheese goes extremely well on these burgers in place of the Cheddar.

New Mexico Burgers

NEW MEXICO BURGERS

prep time **10** mins   cook time **16** mins   serves **6** people   Jan Muller   b e e f

Who says that a burger needs a bun? These spicy creations are served in a flour tortilla with all the fixings of a burrito. For even more spice, try making them with shredded pepper-jack cheese in place of the Mexican cheese blend!

SHOPPING LIST

6 (8-ounce) hamburger patties

vegetable oil

1 ½ cups **shredded Mexican cheese blend**

6 flour tortillas

1 ½ cups **guacamole**

2 cups shredded **iceberg lettuce**

½ cup diced **red onion**

½ cup diced **tomatoes**

1 jalapeño pepper, seeded and minced

1 cup **sour cream**

1. Lightly oil or spray a grill or indoor grill pan, and then heat on high.

2. Place burgers on grill, grill 6 to 8 minutes, flip, and grill for another 6 to 8 minutes for medium, depending on your grill.

3. Place a generous amount of shredded cheese on burgers, heating to melt.

4. Remove burgers from grill, and serve in a flour tortilla topped with guacamole. Serve shredded lettuce, onion, tomato, jalapeño, and sour cream on the side.

HELPFUL TIPS

When buying pre-made burgers in bulk, vacuum seal any extra patties individually to prevent freezer burn.

Spicy Mac-Daddy Burgers

prep time **10** mins   cook time **16** mins   serves **6** people   Bob Warden

You may need to warn your guests that this is one spicy burger! With jalapeño peppers and minced onion mixed right into the Thousand Island dressing slathered over each side of the bun, this recipe really brings the heat. Keep a little of the regular Thousand Island dressing around for those that aren't up to the challenge!

Shopping List

6 (8-ounce) **hamburger patties**

vegetable oil

2 cups **Thousand Island dressing**

2 **jalapeño peppers**, seeded and minced

¼ cup minced **red onion**

6 **sesame seed buns**

6 leaves **romaine lettuce**, cut in half across the vein

12 slices **tomato**

24 slices **dill pickle**

1. Lightly oil or spray a grill or indoor grill pan, and then heat on high.

2. Place burgers on grill, grill 6 to 8 minutes, flip, and grill an additional 6 to 8 minutes for medium, depending on your grill.

3. Meanwhile, in a mixing bowl, combine the Thousand Island dressing, jalapeño peppers, and minced red onion.

4. Spread sauce on inside of buns, both top and bottom, and place 2 halves of romaine lettuce and 2 slices of tomato on each crown.

5. Remove burgers from grill, place in bun, and top with 4 slices of pickle. Serve immediately.

Helpful Tips

Jalapeño peppers freeze beautifully. Seeding them prior to vacuum sealing is the trick to making them easy to work with once defrosted.

NEW YORK STRIP STEAK

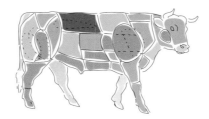

Also known in America as the Kansas City steak, the New York strip steak is prized by steak lovers and is often one of the most expensive cuts of meat. When on sale, pre-cut strip steaks can be purchased in large family packs at your local supermarket to take advantage of the savings, but the biggest savings come when purchasing the whole strip. When purchasing whole, you can get the cost into a more affordable, single digit price per pound. Most whole strip steaks sold in bulk by warehouse clubs average about 6 to 8 pounds and can usually be purchased at a savings of at around 40% when compared to the cost of individual steaks.

Vacuum sealed whole strips can usually be kept refrigerated for up to 10 days if they have a good "sell by" date when you purchase. Vacuum sealing and freezing will keep it good for an entire year. If you are not planning on vacuum sealing right away, you should divide and prepare it for storage within 2 to 3 days of purchase.

Whole strip steaks may need to be trimmed of excess fat. A boning knife is perfect for this purpose. A whole strip steak is usually around 18 inches long and can be cut into individual steaks as thick as you desire. If vacuum sealing, we recommend you cut the steaks to your desired thickness and weight before freezing, as the thawing time will be far, far less than if left whole. A long chef's knife is all you should need for cutting the steaks. A ruler can be used to pre-mark your strip to insure that you get uniform thickness and don't get left with a piece that is too thin to be a steak. You definitely want to prepare your entire strip as steaks!

Many chefs consider it a crime to marinate a strip steak and we agree. Strip steaks have one of the most unique tastes of any cut of meat, and marinating overpowers this subtle but distinct flavor.

Strip steaks are best prepared medium-rare to medium, and are amazingly tender. However, overcooking them to medium-well to well will make them very tough and is definitely not recommended. If you like your steak cooked more than medium, your money would be better spent buying a cheaper cut of meat such as a tri tip or flank steak, as they better hold their flavor and tenderness when cooked to medium-well or well done.

CONTENTS

Cobb Salad with Strip Steak in a New York Minute

Cobb Salad with Strip Steak in a New York Minute

prep time **25** mins · cook time **14** mins · serves **8** people · Bob Warden

The Cobb salad is said to have originated in the kitchens of the Hollywood Brown Derby. Most people finely chop their Cobb salad, but I like mine cut larger, as it is a lot less work and makes for a nice presentation.

1. Place oven rack at the highest position and preheat broiler.

2. Brush steaks with reserved bacon grease and season generously with salt and pepper.

3. Place steaks on broiler pan and place under broiler. Broil for 5 to 7 minutes, flip steaks, and broil for another 5 to 7 minutes for medium rare doneness.

4. Remove the steaks to a cutting board, let rest for 10 minutes, and then slice thinly.

Shopping List

4 (**12**-ounce) **New York strip steaks**

12 slices **bacon**, cooked and crumbled, grease reserved

salt and **pepper**

3 cups torn **romaine lettuce**

3 cups thinly sliced **iceberg lettuce**

6 **plum tomatoes**, quartered

2 **avocados**, peeled, pitted, and thinly sliced

6 **eggs**, hardboiled, quartered

3 tablespoons chopped **chives**

1 ½ cups **blue cheese dressing**

5. Assemble remaining ingredients into 8 salads, topping each with an equal amount of the sliced steak. Serve with blue cheese dressing on the side.

Helpful Tips

You can also serve the salad family style, preparing one large salad and serving alongside a platter of the steak at the table for guests to serve themselves.

LIME AND PEPPERCORN KISSED NEW YORK STRIP STEAK

b
e
e
f

prep time **15** mins · cook time **12** mins · serves **4** people · Bob Warden

Lemons get most of the attention in the kitchen, but I absolutely love the flavor of lime on a nice cut of meat. Using both the juice and the zest in the preparation ensures that you'll get every bit of flavor out of the lime and onto the plate, just where I want it!

SHOPPING LIST

4 (**10**-ounce) **New York strip steaks**

2 tablespoons **course ground black peppercorn**

1 lime, zested and juiced

salt

1. Lightly oil or spray a grill or indoor grill pan, and then heat on high.

2. In a food processor, pulse together the course ground peppercorns and the lime zest.

3. Generously season steaks with salt and coat one side of each steak with the peppercorn and lime zest mixture.

4. Place steaks on hot grill, grill for 2-3 minutes, turn 45 degrees, and grill for 2 additional minutes. Flip steaks, grill for 2-3 minutes, turn 45 degrees, and grill 2 additional minutes.

5. Transfer steaks to a section of the grill with medium heat, drizzle the lime juice over top, and continue to cook for 2 final minutes for medium rare. Serve immediately.

HELPFUL TIPS

A fresh lime is an absolute must for this recipe. Lime juice, more than lemon juice, just does not taste the same from a bottle.

New York Strip Steak with Herbed Cheese Sauce

prep time **15** mins · cook time **25** mins · serves **4** people · Jan Muller

Herbed cheese spreads such as Boursin are usually lighter and fluffier than cream cheese and come in a variety of flavors, but for this dish I prefer those that have garlic in them as it adds a lot more flavor to the final dish.

1. Add 1 tablespoon of the butter to a sauté pan over high heat.

2. Generously season steaks with salt and pepper and place in hot pan. Cook for 3-4 minutes on each side for medium rare doneness. Transfer to a plate and cover with foil to keep warm.

3. Add red wine to the hot pan and boil until reduced by ⅔.

Shopping List

4 (10-ounce) **New York strip steaks**

2 tablespoons **butter**

salt and **pepper**

¼ cup **red wine**

¾ cup **heavy cream**

¾ cup **herbed cheese spread** (such as Boursin)

¼ cup chopped **scallions**

2 tablespoons chopped **fresh chives**

4. Add heavy cream, reduce heat to low, and simmer until heavy cream is reduced by ½.

5. Whisk in herbed cheese spread and scallions, continuing to whisk until the cheese is entirely melted. Whisk in the remaining 1 tablespoon of butter.

6. Serve steaks topped with the hot cheese sauce and sprinkled with the fresh chopped chives.

Helpful Tips

Herbed cheese spreads are usually sold in small tubs in either the imported cheese case or below the bags of shredded cheese in the regular cheese case. For a cheaper alternative, you can also use an herb or chive flavored cream cheese spread, usually sold in tubs alongside the regular cream cheese.

Cuban Spiced New York Strip Steaks with Honey Adobo Sauce

Cuban Spiced New York Strip Steaks with Honey Adobo Sauce

prep time **25** mins   cook time **15** mins   serves **4** people   Jan Muller

beef

This recipe calls for honey adobo sauce; the word adobo being a Spanish word used to refer to a sauce, seasoning, or marinade. Nice premade Mexican and Cuban sauces and marinades are sold in most grocery stores nowadays. They have a bit of a bite, so if you prefer a milder sauce, Chimichurri sauce is also a very good choice.

1. Lightly oil or spray a grill or indoor grill pan, and then heat on high.

2. Combine all dry rub ingredients. Generously season steaks with salt and pepper, and coat one side of each steak with dry rub.

3. Place steaks on hot grill and grill for 4 to 5 minutes on each side.

Shopping List

4 (**10**-ounce) **New York strip steaks**

salt and **pepper**

2 cups **honey adobo sauce** (or other "adobo" sauce/marinade)

Dry Rub

2 tablespoons **chili powder**

1 tablespoon **paprika**

1 tablespoon **ground coriander**

1 tablespoon **ground mustard**

1 ½ teaspoons **dry oregano**

1 ½ teaspoons **cumin**

4. Transfer steaks to a section of the grill with medium heat, and continue to cook for an additional 2-4 minutes for medium rare doneness.

5. Serve immediately with the honey adobo sauce on the side.

Helpful Tips

Be sure to only use the rub on one side of the steaks, as you do not want to completely overpower the natural taste of the meat.

NEW YORK STRIP STEAK AND MUSHROOMS IN CREAM SAUCE

prep time **15** mins   cook time **35** mins   serves **4** people   Jan Muller

This recipe is just like the classic dish Steak Diane, though that is usually prepared with cubed beef tenderloin and not New York strip. My recipe keeps the strip steaks whole to ensure that they do not overcook as easily as cubed meat.

1. Add 1 tablespoon of the butter to a sauté pan over high heat.

2. Generously season steaks with salt and pepper and place in hot pan. Cook for 3-4 minutes on each side for medium rare doneness. Transfer to a plate and cover with foil to keep warm.

3. Melt remaining 1 tablespoon of butter in the hot pan, add mushrooms, and cook for 7 to 10 minutes to brown. Add minced garlic and cook for another 3 to 4 minutes. Transfer to the plate of steaks and re-cover.

SHOPPING LIST

4 (10-ounce) **New York strip steaks**

2 tablespoons **butter**, unsalted

salt and **pepper**

2 pounds **whole mushrooms**

3 cloves **garlic**, minced

½ cup **heavy cream**

2 teaspoons **Worcestershire sauce**

¼ cup **beef stock**

½ teaspoon chopped **fresh rosemary**

½ teaspoon chopped **fresh thyme**

4. Add heavy cream and Worcestershire sauce to the hot pan, and cook 3-4 minutes or until slightly thickened.

5. Add beef stock, rosemary, and thyme, and whisk. Return steak, mushrooms, and garlic to the pan, cover, and cook for 5 minutes, just until steaks are hot. Serve steaks smothered with mushrooms and sauce from the pan.

HELPFUL TIPS

If you decide to go with the cubed version, make extra, and vacuum seal and freeze portions for later. When you need dinner fast, just drop the frozen bags into boiling water for 15-20 minutes, and dinner is ready.

PRIME RIB

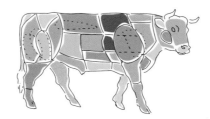

Prime rib is not named after the USDA's 'Prime' quality grade, but instead gets its name from the fact that prime rib constitutes the majority of the primal cut of beef. Prime rib contains large amounts of marbled fat when compared to most other primal cuts, and therefore when roasted, it produces moist and rich flavors.

Whole prime beef ribs are relatively inexpensive when compared to smaller individual roasts. We have found a consistent savings of 40-60 percent when purchased whole. Whole prime rib roasts have the bone-in and can weigh over twenty pounds, so you can cut several small roasts from each.

Vacuum sealed prime ribs can usually be kept refrigerated for up to 10 days if purchased with a good 'sell by' date, or frozen for up to 1 year. If your prime rib is not vacuum sealed, you should divide and/or prepare it for storage within 2 or 3 days of purchase.

Whole prime ribs may need to be trimmed of excess fat. A boning knife is perfect for this purpose. You only need to leave a cap of about a ½ inch to keep the roast perfectly moist. You can cut crisscross hatching into this fat about ¼ inch deep to encourage the fat to melt off, and make for a crispy, crunchy crust. If you wish, you can separate the rib bones from the rib eye for a boneless, rib eye roast. The prime rib bones are quite meaty and can be served as barbecue beef ribs or even braised like short ribs. In fact,

short ribs are taken from the short end of the prime rib. Of course, the standing rib roast is the king of roasts for the special occasion, so leave the bones in when you want rave reviews.

The most unique recipe in this section is the Prime Rib Baked in a Salt Crust. If you have never cooked meat, chicken, or fish in a salt crust, you have to try this recipe. It's really easy, and we promise that you will be amazed at how juicy and flavorful the roast turns out. We also promise you that you remove the salt before serving!

CONTENTS

Cracked Black Pepper and Herb Prime Rib with Mushroom Sauce

CRACKED BLACK PEPPER AND HERB PRIME RIB WITH MUSHROOM SAUCE

prep time **10** mins cook time **5+** hrs serves **8+** people Jan Muller

When I have the time, I always slow roast my prime rib roasts. Slow roasting makes a huge difference with a prime rib, as you get less shrinkage and the roast is so succulent that you will wish you always had the time to cook it this way.

1. Preheat oven to 250 degrees. Heat a large sauté pan over high heat.

2. Rub prime rib with oil, salt, and pepper. Place in the hot sauté pan, brown on all sides, and transfer to roasting pan.

3. Cool roast, and rub on garlic, rosemary, and tarragon. Place in hot oven, and bake for 5 hours for medium doneness.

4. Meanwhile, add mushrooms to a hot sauté pan and brown.

5. In a bowl, whisk together broth, wine, mustard, cornstarch, and 2 teaspoons of tap water. Add mixture to the mushrooms, and simmer 5 minutes, or until thickened. Reserve until roast is finished.

6. Transfer roast to a cutting board and let rest 15 minutes. Meanwhile, skim fat off drippings and add drippings to the sauce. Reheat sauce, slice roast, and serve together.

SHOPPING LIST

1 **boneless prime rib**, about **5** pounds

2 tablespoons **olive oil**

1 tablespoon **salt**

2 tablespoons **cracked black pepper**

8 cloves **garlic**, minced

2 tablespoons minced **fresh rosemary**

2 tablespoons minced **fresh tarragon**

1 pound **mushrooms**, sliced

1 cup **beef broth** or **stock**

¾ cup **red wine**

1 tablespoon **Dijon mustard**

2 teaspoons **cornstarch**

HELPFUL TIPS

At the end of the meal, I pack the left over slices of beef in the sauce, and vacuum seal and freeze it. Then on a night when I get home late from work, I just drop the bag in boiling water, and in 20 minutes I can assemble the world's best hot beef sandwich!

Simple Prime Rib with Au Jus

prep time (5) mins   cook time (3) hrs   serves (8+) people   Bob Warden

Years ago this was my first prime rib effort, and for Thanksgiving Day, no less! Thankfully, it turned out to be a delicious hit and has been a staple in my repertoire ever since. If you've ever had a great slice of prime rib with au jus in a restaurant and wondered how to make it at home, wonder no more!

Shopping List

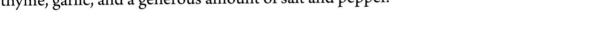

1 **boneless prime rib**, about **5** pounds

2 tablespoons **olive oil**

1 teaspoon **dry thyme**

1 teaspoon **granulated garlic**

salt and **pepper**

3 cups **beef broth** or **stock**

1. Preheat oven to 375 degrees.

2. Rub roast with oil, and then sprinkle it with thyme, garlic, and a generous amount of salt and pepper.

3. Place roast in a roasting pan, add beef broth, place in oven, and roast 3 hours for medium doneness.

4. Transfer roast to a cutting board, let rest 15 minutes, carve, and serve with Au Jus from pan.

HELPFUL TIPS

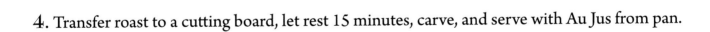

For even more flavor, add rosemary to the rub mixture, and then vacuum seal the prime rib, letting it marinate in your refrigerator overnight before roasting.

GARLIC LOVERS ROASTED GARLIC PRIME RIB

prep time **5** mins cook time **3½** hrs serves **8+** people Bob Warden

A garlic lover's feast that is quick and easy to prepare! Whenever I have a bunch of garlic heads, I roast and then vacuum seal them. That way I have roasted garlic for things like this roast, or for simple garlic bread without the bite of using unroasted, fresh garlic.

SHOPPING LIST

1 **boneless prime rib**, about 5 pounds

4 heads **garlic**

1 cup **olive oil**

salt and **pepper**

1. Preheat oven to 350 degrees.

2. Cut tops off heads of garlic, place upside down on a baking dish, and pour olive oil over top. Bake for 1 hour.

3. Cool garlic slightly, and then squeeze roasted garlic cloves from bulbs, transferring to a food processor and pulsing to form a paste. Add 4 tablespoons of the olive oil the garlic was roasted in to the food processor, and pulse until smooth.

4. Generously season prime rib with salt and pepper and rub with roasted garlic paste. Place prime rib in roasting pan, put in oven, and roast for 2 ½ hours for medium-rare to medium doneness.

5. Transfer roast to a cutting board, let rest 15 minutes, carve, and serve.

HELPFUL TIPS

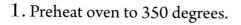

For even more roasted garlic flavor, vacuum seal the prime rib after rubbing on the roasted garlic, and refrigerate for up to 24 hours prior to cooking.

Kosher Salt Encrusted Prime Rib

Kosher Salt Encrusted Prime Rib

prep time **15** mins · cook time **2½** hrs · serves **8+** people · Jan and Bob

This is not only the most delicious prime rib dish I have found, but also, a very interesting roast to pull out of the oven in front of guests. The first time I had a roast like this at a friend's house all I could think was that it would taste like one big salt lick, but in the end, all I wanted to lick was my plate, it was that delicious.

Shopping List

1 **boneless prime rib**, about **5** pounds

2 (**1**-ounce) packets **French onion soup mix**

2 tablespoons minced **fresh rosemary**

1 box **kosher salt**

3 cups **beef broth** or **stock**

1 jar **horseradish cream sauce**, optional

1. Preheat oven to 350 degrees.

2. Place prime rib in a roasting pan and rub with 1 of the packets of French onion soup mix and the rosemary.

3. Mix kosher salt into 1 cup of tap water to make a paste and pack the paste around the prime rib.

4. Bake roast for 2 ½ hours for medium rare to medium doneness.

5. Bring beef broth to a boil, add the other packet of French onion soup mix, and simmer 10 minutes.

6. Remove prime rib from oven. Crack the salt crust and remove completely, discarding.

7. Transfer prime rib to a cutting board, let rest 15 minutes, slice, and serve with the simmered French onion broth and horseradish cream sauce, if desired.

Helpful Tips

I would definitely recommend using a meat thermometer to test for doneness. Look for a reading of 130-135 for medium rare or 140-145 for medium.

ROUND ROAST

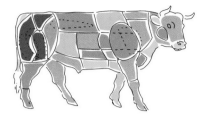

The round is the largest primal cut of beef, and is usually broken down into smaller cuts of top round, bottom round, outside round, and eye round. These cuts can vary greatly in size. We have found that the top round is usually available in bulk packages weighing around 10 to 12 pounds. This large of a package definitely needs to be broken down into smaller packages, unless you are planning a party for 25 or more (and if you are, we wish you luck)!

All of the round cuts, when purchased in large sizes, are often the best price-per-pound bargains in the entire meat case.

Because top round is somewhat tender, it can be cut into steaks that are especially good for pan frying. Now, it also takes well to slow cooking and braising, perfect for roasts and stews. Round steaks are best cut thin for minute steaks, and then tenderized with your favorite tenderizing tool or marinade. The ubiquitous 'Chicken Fried Steak' is most often made from a very tenderized, and then breaded round steak.

We recommend that you cut several roasts and steaks from each round, and then use the smaller pieces for stews, stir-fries, or grinding into ground round... a nice and lean ground beef.

Vacuum sealed whole rounds can usually be kept refrigerated for up to 10 days if purchased with a good 'sell by' date, or frozen for up to 1 year. If your round is not vacuum sealed, you should divide and/or prepare it for storage within 2 or 3 days of purchase.

Whole rounds may need to be trimmed of excess fat. A boning knife is perfect for this purpose. When cutting steaks from a round, be sure to cut across the grain or you may have a pretty chewy steak.

In this section, we offer you a very special Pot Roast German Style that is cooked in beer. Jan and I came up with the recipe after finding a few old bottles of German beer in his cellar. He had no idea when he bought the beer, but the roast was delicious!

CONTENTS

ROUND ROAST DONE EASY

prep time **5** mins   cook time **3** hrs   serves **8** people   Bob Warden

When someone told me about this particular 'roasting' method—starting at a high temperature and then simply turning the oven off to finish baking through residual heat—I was skeptical, but it really works! I like to include aromatic ingredients like the onion and garlic used in this dish to enhance the flavor of the beef.

SHOPPING LIST

1 **round roast**, about **3** pounds

3 tablespoons **olive oil**

salt and **pepper**

6 cloves **garlic**, peeled

1 **large onion**, quartered

1. Preheat oven to 500 degrees. Add 2 tablespoons of the oil to a sauté pan over high heat.

2. Generously season roast with salt and pepper and add to the hot pan, searing until browned on at least 2 sides.

3. Transfer roast to a roasting pan and surround with garlic and onion.

4. Place roast in oven and then immediately reduce heat to 475 degrees; bake for 30 minutes.

5. Turn off oven, but do not remove roast. Let the roast continue to bake in the residual heat of the oven for an additional 2 ½ hours without opening oven. Transfer roast to a cutting board, slice, and serve.

HELPFUL TIPS

I have found that tying a colorful towel to the oven door helps to remind everyone, including myself, to not open the oven door.

Beef and Vegetable Stir Fry

BEEF AND VEGETABLE STIR FRY

prep time **15** mins   cook time **15** mins   serves **8** people   Jan Muller

Stir-fries are so quick to prepare and cook, especially if you buy your vegetables already pre-cut. Based on your preferences, feel free to switch out the vegetables used in this dish with others such as shitake mushrooms, baby corn, or slices of squash, zucchini, or eggplant.

1. Heat 1 tablespoon of the oil in a sauté pan over high heat.

2. In a bowl, whisk together cornstarch, sugar, soy sauce, and beef broth. Toss the strips of beef in ¼ of this sauce and reserve remaining sauce for later.

3. Add broccoli, carrots, snap peas, and red onion to the hot pan and cook for 4-5 minutes. Add water chestnuts and cook for 1 additional minute. Remove vegetables from pan and cover with foil to keep them warm.

4. Add remaining tablespoon of oil and the coated meat to the hot pan and cook for 4-5 minutes.

SHOPPING LIST

2 pounds **round roast**, cut into strips

2 tablespoons **vegetable oil**

¼ cup **cornstarch**

¼ cup **sugar**

¾ cup **soy sauce**, regular or reduced sodium

½ cup **beef broth** or **stock**

5 cups **broccoli florets**

4 cups sliced **carrots**

2 cups **sugar snap peas**

1 cup chopped **red onion**

1 can sliced **water chestnuts**, drained

cooked white rice

5. Add the reserved sauce and stir-fried vegetables to the pan, reduce the heat to low, cover, and simmer another 4 minutes. Serve over cooked rice.

HELPFUL TIPS

If you plan to vacuum seal and freeze this dish, stop after browning the meat in step 4. Then simply toss everything, including sauce, into the vacuum seal bag, seal, and freeze. To serve, thaw over night in your refrigerator, and then pick up again at step 5, adding a few more minutes to your cook time.

Pot Roast German Style

Pot Roast German Style

prep time **20** mins — cook time **2** hrs — serves **8** people — Jan and Bob

Now, I don't actually know if they make a beer simmered pot roast like this in Germany, but I do know that they love beer! Not a beer lover? Try substituting coke or root beer for the beer in this recipe.

1. Add butter to a Dutch oven over high heat. Generously season roast with salt and pepper and add to hot pan, browning on at least 2 sides. Remove from pan and reserve.

2. Add cut onion and celery to hot pan and cook for 5 minutes to brown. Remove from pan and reserve.

3. Reduce heat to medium, add garlic and remaining diced vegetables to hot pan, and cook 10 minutes to soften.

Shopping List

1 round roast, about **3** pounds

3 tablespoons **butter**

salt and **pepper**

1 large onion, cut into sixths

4 stalks **celery**, cut into **1** inch lengths

2 cloves **garlic**, minced

1 large onion, diced

4 stalks **celery**, diced

2 cups **beef broth** or **stock**

1 (12-ounce) can or bottle **beer**

1 bay leaf

4. Return the browned cut vegetables to pan and place roast on top of vegetables.

5. Add beef broth, beer, and bay leaf to the pan and bring to a simmer. Cover and simmer for 1 ½ hours, or until roast is fork tender. Let rest 15 minutes before slicing. Season vegetables and pan juices with salt and pepper to taste and serve over top roast.

Helpful Tips

Add shredded cabbage, or even sauerkraut to this recipe to give it an even more German feel.

SOUPED UP SLOW COOKER ROUND ROAST

prep time **10** mins   cook time **6+** hrs   serves **8** people   Bob Warden

This is the perfect roast for any mushroom and onion lovers. If, as a mushroom and onion lover, you have some vacuum sealed and frozen on hand, you can certainly use them for this recipe as they'll work fine, and you don't even need to thaw them!

SHOPPING LIST

1 **round roast**, about **3** pounds

1 (**10.75**-ounce) can **condensed cream of mushroom soup**

1 (**1**-ounce) packet **powdered onion soup mix**

1 ½ cups **beef broth** or **stock**

pepper

1 **large onion**, thickly sliced

1 pound **button mushrooms**, thickly sliced

1. In a bowl, whisk together cream of mushroom soup, onion soup mix, and beef broth, and then pour into a slow cooker.

2. Generously season roast with pepper and place it in slow cooker. Top with onion and mushrooms, and set slow cooker to low.

3. Cook 6-7 hours, or until roast is fork tender.

4. Remove roast to a cutting board and let rest 15 minutes before slicing and serving topped with sauce and vegetables.

HELPFUL TIPS

Serve this right over a big mound of mashed potatoes, or even over buttered egg noodles like a stroganoff.

STEW MEAT

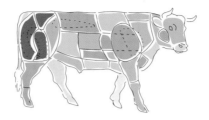

Most stew meat is sold pre-cut into 1 to 1 ½ inch pieces. The stew meat usually available in bulk or family packs, is cut from the bottom round. Occasionally, the butcher may use trimmings from other primal cuts of beef, and the label may or may not indicate what cut or cuts were used. We have found that warehouse clubs almost always use bottom round. Although this is a tough cut of beef, it can become remarkably tender when slow cooked or braised in stews and soups.

The first key to developing flavor with stew meats is to brown the individual pieces. This will develop complex flavor compounds that you simply will not get by throwing the meat straight into stewing liquid. When browning stew meat, use a thick-bottomed sauté pan over medium-high heat. Never crowd the meat in the pan or the meat will steam, rather than brown. We like to leave as much space between meat pieces as the pieces themselves. Although it takes time, we recommend that you turn the pieces on all sides with a pair of tongs to evenly brown. Once finished, remove the browned pieces of stew meat, set them aside, and deglaze the pan using the cooking liquid suggested in the recipe you are preparing: usually wine, broth, or water.

The second key to developing flavor with stew meat is entirely dependent on the quality of the cooking liquids used, the herbs, spices, and other ingredients that season the meat as it cooks. Fresh herbs and spices make a huge difference in flavor. When using dried herbs and spices, make sure that they are not more than six months old, and have been stored in airtight containers to preserve their flavor.

The key to tender stew meat is long, slow cooking. 3 to 5 hours on the stovetop, oven, or slow cooker; or 60 to 90 minutes in a pressure cooker should give you nice and tender results. Just remember, stew meat only gets more tender as it stews (which is good, but sometimes bad)! A fork inserted into the meat should meet only slight resistance. Properly cooked stew meat should remain intact and not fall apart when handled gently. If the pieces do fall apart or are stringy, they are overcooked. If the finished pieces are tough, they are probably undercooked, or were cooked at too high of a temperature. The best temperature is the one that will keep the liquid in the pot or baking dish at a slow simmer, and nothing more.

At one time, Jan and I counted over 1,000 different stew recipes in our combined recipe books. Here are 4 of our favorites.

CONTENTS

beef

CREAMY BEEF STEW WITH READY BAKE BISCUITS

prep time	cook time	serves	Bob Warden
30 mins	**2+** hrs	**8** people	

This extra creamy beef stew looks best when topped with golden biscuits as is written in the recipe; however, I actually like to place two biscuits at the bottom of my bowl and ladle the stew over top, letting them really soak in the broth.

1. Add butter to a Dutch oven over high heat.

2. Generously season stew meat with salt and pepper and then toss in the flour until evenly coated.

3. Sear the stew meat in the hot pot, until browned. (You may need to do this in batches.)

4. In a bowl, whisk together cream of mushroom soup, gravy, beef broth, tomato paste, paprika and bay leaf. Add to the hot pot, bring up to a boil, reduce heat to low, and add onion, carrots, and celery.

5. Cover and let simmer for 1-2 hours, or until meat is fork tender.

SHOPPING LIST

2 pounds **stew meat**, cubed

4 tablespoons **butter**

salt and **pepper**

¼ cup **flour**

1 (**10.75**-ounce) can **condensed cream of mushroom soup**

1 (**10.25**-ounce) can **brown gravy**

2 cups **beef broth** or **stock**

3 tablespoons **tomato paste**

1 teaspoon **paprika**

1 bay leaf

½ cup largely diced **onion**

½ cup sliced **carrots**

½ cup largely chopped **celery**

2 cans **ready to bake biscuits**

6. Cook biscuits according to the directions on the package. Season stew with salt and pepper to taste and serve each bowl topped with 2 of the baked biscuits.

HELPFUL TIPS

If you egg wash your biscuits prior to baking, you will get a beautiful shine and a richer color when they come out of the oven.

BEEF STEW COOKED REAL SLOW

prep time **30** mins   cook time **10+** hrs   serves **8** people   Jan Muller   beef

While you are out of the house all day, this stew will be filling your kitchen with its delicious aroma. What a nice way to end the day! (And hey… only having to start the day with this recipe's simple 3 step preparation isn't too bad either!)

SHOPPING LIST

2 pounds **stew meat**, cubes

salt and **pepper**

¼ cup **flour**

2 cups largely chopped **red bliss potatoes**

2 cups largely chopped **parsnips**

2 cups **baby carrots**

1 cup chopped **onion**

1 cup cut **celery**, in **1** inch lengths

1 teaspoon **paprika**

1 teaspoon **Worcestershire sauce**

6 cups **beef broth** or **stock**

1 **bay leaf**

1. Generously season stew meat with salt and pepper and then toss in the flour until evenly coated.

2. Place coated meat and all other ingredients into the slow cooker.

3. Cover and cook on low for 10-12 hours, or until meat is fork tender. Season with salt and pepper to taste and serve immediately.

HELPFUL TIPS

If you buy small red bliss potatoes, you will only have to cut them in half before adding them to the stew. Less prep-work is always good!

Southwest Beef and Vegetable Stew

Southwest Beef and Vegetable Stew

prep time **30** mins cook time **2-3** hrs serves **8** people Jan Muller

beef

Generally, Mexican stews start with fully cooked meats, which are combined with the various liquids and vegetables, but this recipe makes it all from scratch in one pot. Top with a shredded Mexican cheese blend, if desired.

1. Add the olive oil to a Dutch oven over high heat.

2. Generously season stew meat with salt and pepper. Add seasoned meat, onion, and peppers to the hot pot and cook until meat has browned and vegetables are soft. (You may need to do this in batches.)

3. Whisk together ¼ cup of tap water, diced tomatoes, picante sauce, cumin, and garlic powder. Add mixture to the hot pot.

4. Bring mixture up to a boil, reduce heat to low, and simmer for 1 hour.

SHOPPING LIST

2 pounds **stew meat**, cubed

¼ cup **olive oil**

salt and **pepper**

1 cup diced **onion**

1 cup diced **bell peppers**, any color

3 (**10**-ounce) cans **diced tomatoes with green chilies**, with juice

1 cup **picante sauce**

1 teaspoon **cumin**

½ teaspoon **garlic powder**

2 cups **frozen corn**

1 (15-ounce) can **black beans**, drained and rinsed

5. Stir in the corn and black beans and simmer for an additional 1-2 hours, or until meat is fork tender. Serve immediately.

HELPFUL TIPS

You can serve this stew with bread, but personally, I recommend serving it with tortilla chips instead so that you can scoop up bites of stew.

CLASSIC BEEF STEW

prep time **30** mins   cook time **2+** hrs   serves **8** people   Bob Warden

This is the everyday preparation of beef stew that I've been preparing for as long as I can remember. The instant rice is not only a great ingredient in this, but its starch also helps thicken the final dish.

SHOPPING LIST

2 pounds **stew meat**, cubed

4 tablespoons **butter**

salt and **pepper**

¼ cup **flour**

6 cups **beef broth** or **stock**

4 cups diced **Idaho potatoes**

2 cups diced **carrots**

1 **bay leaf**

2 tablespoons chopped **fresh rosemary**

1 cup frozen **corn kernels**

1 cup frozen **green beans**

¼ cup **instant rice**

1. Add butter to a Dutch oven over high heat.

2. Generously season stew meat with salt and pepper and then toss in the flour until evenly coated.

3. Sear the stew meat in the hot pot, until browned. (You may need to do this in batches.)

4. Add beef broth, potatoes, carrots, and bay leaf. Cover and cook for 1-2 hours, or until meat is fork tender.

5. Uncover and add rosemary, corn, green beans, and instant rice and cook for an additional 10 minutes.

6. Season with salt and pepper to taste, ladle into bowls, and serve immediately.

HELPFUL TIPS

As a healthier alternative to the rice, you can also try substituting barley. It has an earthier flavor that definitely adds another layer to the dish.

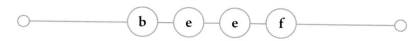

Top Sirloin

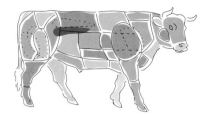

Top sirloin is cut from just behind the t-bone cut and just below the tenderloin of the cow, so that may explain why it is one of the most popular cuts of meat in restaurants. With a great flavor, texture, and just the right amount of fat, you'd be hard pressed to find a better steak for grilling that can come anywhere near the price-per-pound. Just be sure that the package says 'top' sirloin before purchasing, as ordinary 'sirloin' is a nearby, but entirely different cut of meat that is not nearly as prized.

Bulk packages of top sirloin roasts can be purchased in warehouse clubs and cut into top sirloin steaks for a fraction of the price of purchasing the steaks pre-cut in a grocery store. That said, you can still get a good deal on family packs of cut top sirloin steaks in ordinary grocery stores or big box retailers, especially when they go on sale. Keep an eye out around summer grilling holidays like the 4th of July for the best sale prices on top sirloin and other grilling staples (like ground beef, to name the obvious). As ordinary grocery stores fight for your business on super competitive holidays, you may momentarily be able to save more money than even buying the same cuts of meat at a warehouse club. Of course, keep an eye out for the warehouse club's sales around that time as well! Use the opportunity to purchase as much as you are comfortable storing, vacuum seal, and freeze to spread the savings out for months to come.

Whole sirloin roasts can be kept whole for roasting, or cut into individual sirloin steaks before vacuum sealing for a much quicker thawing time.

Vacuum sealed top sirloin can usually be kept refrigerated for up to 10 days if purchased with a good 'sell by' date, or frozen for up to 1 year. If your top sirloin is not vacuum sealed, you should divide and/or prepare it for storage within 2 or 3 days of purchase.

In this section, we highly recommend the Grilled Marinated Top Sirloin Steaks, as it is simply one of the absolute best ways to prepare a top sirloin steak, playing off all of the delicious strengths of this cut of meat.

CONTENTS

GRILLED MARINATED TOP SIRLOIN STEAKS

prep time **15** mins   cook time **15** mins   serves **4** people   Jan Muller

This marinated steak uses thyme, which is a very strong herb, so keep in mind that a little goes a long way. Also, thyme is one of those rare herbs where the fresh version is just as potent as the dry, which is nice since it is also one of the easier herbs to grow.

1. In a bowl, whisk together all marinade ingredients.

2. Seal steaks and marinade in a vacuum seal bag and refrigerate overnight.

3. Remove steaks from marinade and let rest for 30 minutes as excess liquid drains. Generously season steaks with salt and pepper.

4. Lightly oil or spray a grill or indoor grill pan, and then heat on high.

SHOPPING LIST

4 (8-ounce) **top sirloin steaks**

salt and **pepper**

MARINADE

2 tablespoons minced **onion**

1 tablespoon minced **garlic**

1 teaspoon minced **fresh thyme**

1 tablespoon **olive oil**

2 tablespoons **Worcestershire sauce**

2 tablespoons **cider vinegar**

2 tablespoons **red wine vinegar**

1 tablespoon **light brown sugar**

5. Place steaks on the hot grill, and grill for 4 to 6 minutes on each side.

6. Transfer steak to a section of the grill with medium heat, and continue to cook for an additional 2 to 3 minutes for medium rare doneness. Serve immediately.

HELPFUL TIPS

If you only have one of the two vinegars in this recipe in your pantry, you can simply double up on that one and skip the other, as they are both sweet vinegars.

TOP SIRLOIN ROAST THE SLOW COOKER WAY

prep time **30** mins   cook time **7-9** hrs   serves **10+** people   Bob Warden

Dry mixes are a quick way to season large cuts of meat, and when done in a slow cooker, the flavors penetrate deep into the meat for an amazingly moist and delicious dish.

1. Add oil to a sauté pan over high heat.

2. Generously season roast with salt and pepper. Sear the roast in the hot pan to brown, and transfer to a slow cooker.

3. In a bowl, whisk together the gravy mix, Italian salad dressing mix, ranch salad dressing mix, and beef broth, and pour mixture over top of the roast.

4. Add onion, celery, and carrot to the slow cooker, cover, and cook on low for 7 to 9 hours.

SHOPPING LIST

1 top **sirloin roast**, 4-5 pounds

2 tablespoons **olive oil**

salt and **pepper**

1 (**1.25**-ounce) packet **powdered brown gravy mix**

1 (**1.25**-ounce) packet **powdered Italian salad dressing mix**

½ (**1.25**-ounce) packet **powdered ranch salad dressing mix**

2 cups **beef broth** or **stock**

2 cups chopped **onion**

1 cup chopped **celery**

1 cup chopped **carrot**

5. Transfer roast from slow cooker to a cutting board, let rest 10 minutes, slice, and serve with a ladle full of the vegetables and broth.

HELPFUL TIPS

I suggest comparing the nutritional information listed on the packets of gravy and dressing mixes and going with those that have the lowest sodium.

TOP SIRLOIN STEAK IN A SWEET ONION SAUCE

prep time **15** mins   cook time **15** mins   serves **4** people   Bob Warden

Grape jelly is the surprise ingredient in this dish, adding only a hint of sweetness that mocks caramelized onions without all the work. Of course, you can also add actual caramelized onions for a dish that is bursting with great onion flavor; simply see my tip at the bottom of the page!

SHOPPING LIST

4 (8-ounce) **top sirloin steaks**

1 tablespoon **olive oil**

salt and **pepper**

1 (10.5-ounce) can **condensed onion soup**

½ cup **beef broth** or **stock**

1 tablespoon **grape jelly**

1. Place a sauté pan over high heat.

2. Rub oil onto steaks and generously season with salt and pepper. Sear steaks in the hot sauté pan for 3 to 4 minutes on each side for medium rare doneness.

3. Remove from pan and cover with aluminum foil to keep warm.

4. In a bowl, whisk together the onion soup, beef broth, and grape jelly.

5. Add onion soup mixture to the hot pan and heat thoroughly. Return steaks to sauté pan and heat for 3 to 5 minutes.

6. Transfer steaks to plates, spoon sauce over top, and serve immediately.

HELPFUL TIPS

The only thing that makes this dish even better is adding actual onions! Simply start by sautéing 1 sliced onion in 1 tablespoon of olive oil until caramelized. Remove and reserve as you cook the steaks. Return the onions to the pan in step 4 and you're all set!

CHICKEN BREASTS

It is estimated that over 40% of recipe searches on the internet are for chicken. The reasons are pretty clear. Chicken is usually the least expensive meat in supermarkets and warehouse clubs. Chicken breasts, though the most expensive cut of chicken, are still inexpensive and lend themselves to hundreds of uses. They are mild enough to allow the world's total variety of herbs, spices, sauces, and marinades to show their full flavors.

Boneless, skinless chicken breasts are the darling of an innumerable amount of low fat recipes. It is simply understood—chicken breasts are probably the best, most lean source of protein on the planet!

A key to cooking chicken breasts is understanding that the thickness entirely dictates the cooking time. It's important to get doneness right, because undercooked chicken is dangerous, and overcooked chicken is rubbery and tough. Recipes usually call for an average sized chicken breast, but nowadays chicken breasts vary in size quite greatly, depending on brand and package. What can you do? You need an instant-read meat thermometer for the best chicken results. With an instant-read thermometer, you can simply remove the chicken from the pan or oven as soon as it reaches 190 degrees, as recommended by the good old USDA.

We have found that chicken breasts purchased in bulk at warehouse clubs typically yield a savings of around 50%. If 40% of your meals include chicken in one form or another, your yearly savings will almost certainly be significant. With savings so high, you can even afford more steaks!

CONTENTS

Spinach, Bacon, and Provolone Stuffed Chicken Breasts

Spinach, Bacon, and Provolone Stuffed Chicken Breasts

prep time **25** mins cook time **45** mins serves **8** people Jan Muller

Stuffing a chicken breast may seem like a lot of work, but the results are not only beautiful, but delicious! These stuffed chicken breasts have bacon on the inside and outside, as you can never really have too much bacon.

Shopping List

8 boneless, skinless chicken breasts

8 slices **bacon**, cooked, crumbled, fat reserved

2 pounds **fresh spinach leaves**

4 cloves **garlic**, minced

½ cup **sour cream**

½ cup shredded **provolone cheese**

salt and **pepper**

16 slices **raw bacon**

1. Preheat oven to 375 degrees. Add reserved bacon fat to a sauté pan and heat on high.

2. Add spinach to the pan and stir gently to wilt; remove and reserve.

3. Add garlic to the hot pan and sauté until soft. Stir in sour cream, provolone cheese, cooled crumbled bacon, and sautéed spinach. Heat through and remove from heat. Season with salt and pepper to taste.

4. Meanwhile cut a pocket into the side of each chicken breast in its thickest part, and then stuff each pocket with spinach mixture.

5. Wrap each chicken breast with 2 slices of bacon in a crisscross fashion, and season generously with salt and pepper.

6. Lay the chicken breasts on a sheet pan with the bacon ends tucked under the breasts and bake for 35 minutes.

7. Turn on broiler and cook for an additional 5 minutes to brown bacon. Serve immediately.

Helpful Tips

To make these without stuffing the chicken, bake the bacon wrapped chicken and then top with the provolone cheese before broiling in step 7. Heat the rest of the stuffing ingredients on the stove and smother the chicken with it as you serve.

Chicken Parmesan

CHICKEN PARMESAN

prep time **20** mins · cook time **23** mins · serves **8** people · Bob Warden

I don't know anyone that doesn't love Chicken Parmesan served with a side of spaghetti. I order it all the time in restaurants, but I have yet to find one that is any better than the one I make myself. (That would be the one in this recipe!)

SHOPPING LIST

8 boneless, skinless chicken breasts

2 tablespoons **butter**

salt and **pepper**

2 cups **Italian breadcrumbs**

½ cup grated **Parmesan cheese**

3 tablespoons minced **fresh parsley**

1 tablespoon **minced garlic**

1 teaspoon **dry basil**

4 large eggs, beaten

4 cups **marinara sauce**

16 slices **mozzarella cheese**, cut into triangles

fresh basil to garnish

1. Add butter to a large sauté pan and heat over medium-high heat.

2. Cut chicken breasts in half to create 2 thin breasts from each. Generously season each with salt and pepper.

3. In a large bowl, combine breadcrumbs, Parmesan cheese, parsley, garlic, and dry basil.

4. Dip chicken into egg, then into breadcrumb mixture.

5. Place breaded chicken in the hot pan, and cook 6-8 minutes on each side.

6. Meanwhile, heat marinara sauce in a separate saucepan until hot and bubbling.

7. Ladle a spoonful of marinara sauce over each piece of breaded chicken and cover with triangles of mozzarella cheese. Sprinkle with additional Parmesan cheese, if desired, and cover pan, just until cheese melts. Serve garnished with fresh basil.

HELPFUL TIPS

Be sure to thoroughly coat the chicken in the breadcrumb mixture, pressing gently to really make it stick.

ASIAN CASHEW CHICKEN

prep time **25** mins   cook time **20** mins   serves **4** people   Bob Warden

Cashew lovers should definitely try this one! This recipe is a simple and easy to make stir-fry, but the cashews are the ingredient that sets things apart. I just love that salty crunch in this dish. Serve with jasmine or basmati rice for a sure crowd pleaser.

1. Add oil to a sauté pan over high heat.

2. Add chicken strips to the hot pan, and stir-fry for 6 to 8 minutes.

3. Add onion, bell pepper, straw mushrooms, and water chestnuts to the hot pan, and stir-fry 5 minutes.

4. Meanwhile, whisk together cornstarch, chicken broth, soy sauce, and ginger.

5. Stir sauce into the hot pan and bring to boil. Continue stirring until sauce thickens.

6. Add cashews, stir, and serve immediately.

SHOPPING LIST

1 pound **boneless, skinless chicken breasts**, cut into strips

2 teaspoons **olive oil**

1 **onion**, chopped

1 **bell pepper**, chopped

1 (6-ounce) can **straw mushrooms**, drained

1 (8-ounce) can **sliced water chestnuts**, drained

2 tablespoons **cornstarch**

⅔ cup **chicken broth**

¼ cup **soy sauce**, regular or reduced sodium

1 teaspoon minced **fresh ginger**

1 cup **roasted cashews**

HELPFUL TIPS

Before serving, finish the dish with a drizzle of sesame oil for an even better flavor!

CHICKEN ENCHILADAS

prep time **25** mins   cook time **45** mins   serves **6** people   Bob Warden

This is a lively Mexican casserole dish that kids love to help prepare (and eat!). Most Mexican dishes require a laundry list of ingredients, but this recipe keeps it simple without skimping on taste.

SHOPPING LIST

2 cups cubed or shredded **cooked chicken breast meat**

1 tablespoon **olive oil**

½ cup sliced **scallions**

1 (4-ounce) can **green chilies**

1 cup **sour cream**

1 cup shredded **Cheddar cheese**

6 (**12** inch) **flour tortillas**

¼ cup **milk**

1. Preheat oven to 350 degrees. Add oil to a sauté pan over medium heat.

2. Add scallions and chilies to the hot pan and sauté until soft. Reduce heat to low and stir in sour cream. Remove ¾ of the mixture from the pan and set aside.

3. Add chicken and ½ cup of the Cheddar cheese to the pan, and heat and stir until mixed well.

4. Fill each of the six tortillas with chicken mixture. Tuck in sides of tortilla rollup and place in a lightly greased 9x13 baking dish, seam side down.

5. Whisk together the milk and the remaining ¾ cup portion of the sour cream mixture. Spoon over rolled tortillas and top with remaining Cheddar cheese.

6. Put baking dish into hot oven and bake for 30 to 35 minutes; the cheese should be bubbling.

HELPFUL TIPS

Since this recipe calls for cooked meat, this is a great way to use leftover chicken!

Barbecued Chicken Ranch Salad

Barbecued Chicken Ranch Salad

prep time **25** mins   cook time **22** mins   serves **8** people   Jan Muller

Corn, black beans, tortilla strips, and a spicy ranch dressing liven up this barbecue chicken salad. This salad is so nice on a hot summer day with a tall cool glass of lemon or limeade.

1. Preheat grill or grill pan to high.

2. Spray grill or grill pan with vegetable oil to prevent sticking.

3. Place chicken breasts on grill and grill 6 to 8 minutes, flip chicken, and grill for another 6 to 8 minutes. Brush with barbecue sauce, grill for another 2 to 3 minutes, flip chicken, brush with barbecue sauce, and grill for another 2 to 3 minutes.

4. Remove chicken from grill and cut into strips.

5. Make the dressing by combining ranch dressing with hot sauce.

Shopping List

4 boneless, skinless chicken breasts

vegetable oil

½ cup **barbecue sauce**

1 head **red leaf lettuce**, cut and cleaned

1 head **romaine lettuce**, cut and cleaned

1 **tomato**, diced

1 bunch **fresh cilantro**, chopped

2 cups **frozen corn kernels**, defrosted and drained

1 (**15.5**-ounce) can **black beans**, drained and rinsed

1 cup **ranch dressing**

6-8 drops **chipotle hot sauce**

tortilla strips, optional

sliced **avocado**, optional

6. Divide lettuce among 8 plates, arrange remaining ingredients on top of lettuce, and finish with tortilla strips and sliced avocado, if desired. Serve dressing on the side.

Helpful Tips

Tobasco brand makes a good chipotle hot sauce that goes great in the dressing. Though I suggest 6-8 drops, use as little or as much as you like!

poultry

ANGEL HAIR PASTA WITH CHICKEN AND BASIL

prep time **15** mins   cook time **20** mins   serves **4** people   Jan Muller

My family loves the light tomato and basil sauce that is created in this chicken and pasta dish. I do not always have the time to make a hearty marinara from scratch, but this quick recipe makes for a nice substitute.

1. Bring a large pot of salted water to a boil.

2. Add oil to a large sauté pan and heat on medium-high.

3. Add onion and garlic to the hot pan and sauté until golden brown, and then reduce heat to medium.

4. Add cooked chicken, tomatoes, and red pepper flakes to the pan. Cover and cook for 5 minutes.

5. Uncover and stir, and then add basil while continuing to stir. Remove from heat, and add salt and pepper to taste.

SHOPPING LIST

4 boneless, skinless chicken breasts, cooked and cubed

2 teaspoons olive oil

1 cup minced onion

4 cloves garlic, minced

6 cups diced tomato

1 teaspoon red pepper flakes

½ cup cut fresh basil, in strips

salt and **pepper**

1 pound angel hair pasta

½ cup shredded provolone cheese

¼ cup shredded Parmesan cheese

6. Cook angel hair pasta as directed on the package, drain pasta, and return it to its pot. Add the sauce, chicken, and provolone cheese to the pasta pot, and stir to thoroughly coat pasta.

7. Divide pasta among 8 plates, and serve with Parmesan cheese and a shaker of red pepper flakes.

HELPFUL TIPS

Angel hair can be a little challenging to cook just right, so you can use spaghetti or any type of pasta if you wish.

CHICKEN BREASTS IN CAPER CREAM

prep time **20** mins · cook time **20** mins · serves **4** people · Jan Muller

'Exquisite' is the word my mother-in-law used the first time she tried this recipe, and she is a women who only gives out culinary compliments when they are deserved. The addition of the capers was an afterthought, but the nice briny flavor really complements the smoothness of the cream sauce.

SHOPPING LIST

4 **boneless, skinless chicken breasts**

3 tablespoons **olive oil**

1 **lemon**, zested and juiced

1 teaspoon minced **fresh dill**

1 teaspoon minced **fresh garlic**

¼ teaspoon **salt**

⅛ teaspoon **pepper**

½ cup **heavy cream**

2 tablespoons **capers**, drained

1. Whisk together 2 tablespoons of the oil, lemon zest and juice, dill, garlic, salt, and pepper. Add marinade and chicken to a vacuum seal bag, and refrigerate for up to 24 hours.

2. Add the remaining tablespoon of oil to a sauté pan and heat on high.

3. Place chicken breasts in the hot pan, sauté for 5 to 7 minutes, flip chicken, and sauté for another 5 to 7 minutes.

4. Reduce heat to low and add heavy cream. Bring to a simmer, cover pan, and cook for 4 to 5 minutes.

5. Uncover, stir in capers, and serve immediately.

HELPFUL TIPS

Watch the heat once you add the cream to avoid curdling it.

Chicken Nuggets Everyone Will Love

CHICKEN NUGGETS EVERYONE WILL LOVE

prep time **20** mins · cook time **20** mins · serves **6** people · Bob Warden

These chicken nuggets put fast food nuggets to shame. It is not just the kids that clamor for these chicken nuggets; you may just find the adults wolfing them down faster than them. I like to have big vacuum sealed bags of these gems already breaded in the freezer for anytime cooking.

SHOPPING LIST

3 boneless, skinless chicken breasts, cut into **1 ½** inch strips

½ cup **butter**

1 cup **breadcrumbs**

½ cup grated **Parmesan cheese**

1 tablespoon **parsley flakes**

1 teaspoon **dry basil**

½ teaspoon **salt**

¼ teaspoon **pepper**

2 large eggs, beaten

1. Add butter to a large sauté pan and heat over medium-high heat to melt butter.

2. Mix together breadcrumbs, Parmesan cheese, parsley flakes, basil, salt, and pepper.

3. Dip chicken pieces in egg, and then dip in breadcrumb mixture.

4. Place breaded chicken in the pan, cook 8 to 10 minutes, flip chicken, and cook for another 8 to 10 minutes.

5. Serve with your favorite dipping sauce.

HELPFUL TIPS

Vegetable oil can be used in place of the butter, but I would suggest adding 1 tablespoon of butter to the oil, just for the added flavor.

Hawaiian Chicken Kabobs

Hawaiian Chicken Kabobs

prep time **25** mins — cook time **25** mins — serves **8** people — Bob Warden

Apple cider vinegar and honey liven up these kabobs for sweet-smelling summer grilling. You can add other seasonal vegetables to these kebobs, but keep the bacon wrapped chicken and the pineapple for sure. I use metal skewers for my kebobs, and I spray them lightly with oil to prevent the food from sticking so it is easier to slide off the skewer when my guests are ready to eat.

1. Whisk soy sauce, cider vinegar, honey, olive oil, and scallions to create a marinade. Place chicken and mushrooms into a vacuum seal bag, cover with marinade, and seal. Refrigerate for up to 24 hours.

2. Lightly oil or spray a grill or indoor grill pan, and then heat on high.

3. Remove chicken from marinade, and then place marinade in a sauce pot, bringing to a boil for 5 minutes.

4. Wrap each chicken chunk with ½ slice bacon, and thread onto a skewer until bacon is securely held in place.

5. Complete skewers by alternating between bacon wrapped chunks of chicken, bell peppers, pineapple, and the marinated mushrooms.

6. Place skewers on hot grill and cook for 10 to 12 minutes. Brush with boiled marinade, flip skewers, and cook for an additional 10 to 12 minutes. Serve immediately.

Shopping List

3 boneless, skinless chicken breasts, cut into **8** chunks each

¼ cup **soy sauce**, regular or reduced sodium

¼ cup **cider vinegar**

2 tablespoons **honey**

2 tablespoons **olive oil**

2 **scallions**, minced

12 mushrooms, or **6** large mushrooms cut in half

9 slices **bacon**, cut in half

2 bell peppers, chopped thickly

½ **pineapple**, cored, skinned, chopped large

skewers

Helpful Tips

If you are using wooden skewers, soak them for several hours in water to help keep them from burning.

p
o
u
l
t
r
y

TANGY GARLIC CHICKEN BREASTS

prep time **20** mins   cook time **30** mins   serves **4** people   Jan Muller

This quick and easy recipe transforms the 'same old chicken' into an impressive gourmet dish. I use button mushrooms in this recipe, but if you feel like splurging, buy fancier varieties like baby bella and use those.

SHOPPING LIST

4 boneless, skinless chicken breasts

2 tablespoons **olive oil**

4 garlic **cloves**, minced

1 pound **mushrooms**, sliced

2 tablespoons **all purpose flour**

¼ cup **balsamic vinegar**

¾ cup **chicken broth** or **stock**

salt and **pepper**

1. Add oil to a sauté pan and heat on high.

2. Place chicken in the hot pan and sauté for 5 to 7 minutes to brown. Flip chicken, sauté for another 5 to 7 minutes to brown, and then remove from the pan and reserve.

3. Add garlic and mushrooms to the hot pan and sauté 5 minutes to brown. Add flour to the pan, stirring to incorporate, and reduce heat.

4. Slowly whisk in vinegar and broth, and bring to a simmer.

5. Return chicken to the pan, cover, and simmer for 10 minutes. Salt and pepper to taste and serve.

HELPFUL TIPS

Add a sprig of fresh rosemary to the pan while simmering in step 5 for an even greater flavor. Serve over pasta or alongside roasted potatoes for a perfect meal.

CHICKEN THIGHS AND LEGS

As mentioned in the previous introduction to chicken breasts, chicken rules the home kitchen, making appearances at 40% of all dinners. Price is a major factor in choosing chicken as a main course ingredient, and chicken thighs and legs are usually the least expensive of the pre-packaged cuts of chicken. We have found that chicken thighs and legs purchased in bulk packs at warehouse clubs typically yield a savings of around 40%. These savings are very significant when you take into account how inexpensive chicken thighs and legs are to begin with!

Chicken thighs and legs have a bold flavor that is all their own. When seasoned with only salt and pepper, they grill up delicious all on their own. The addition of almost any tomato-based sauce, from ketchup to barbecue, sends them into a whole new stratosphere of flavor. Because they have their own, strong flavor (when it comes to chicken), they also stand up well when roasted, broiled, or braised. When breaded and fried, chicken can become a whole fast food chain … or several fast food chains nowadays.

Like all chicken, it is important to handle legs and thighs carefully. Get them home from the market and into the refrigerator right away. If you are not going to cook your bulk purchase within a few days, vacuum seal into smaller packages and freeze. Chicken recipes that call for a marinade may be prepped in advance and the meat frozen with the marinade for easier dinners in the future. They will always be ready to thaw and cook whenever you need them.

We chose the 10 recipes that follow to give you an idea of the variety of ways you can use such a versatile pair of chicken pieces.

CONTENTS

Chicken and Mushroom Fricassee

CHICKEN AND MUSHROOM FRICASSEE

prep time **20** mins   cook time **80** mins   serves **4** people   Bob Warden

Although a fricassee is usually just meat and vegetables stewed in gravy, these chicken legs and crimini mushrooms cook up beautifully in a light, tomato-based Italian gravy that goes great over pasta.

1. Add oil to a large sauté pan and heat on high.

2. Place chicken legs in the hot pan and sauté for 5 to 7 minutes on each side to brown. Remove from pan and reserve.

3. Add mushrooms and garlic to the hot pan, sautéing until mushrooms are soft. Return chicken to the pan and season all generously with salt and pepper.

SHOPPING LIST

8 **chicken legs**

2 tablespoons **olive oil**

1 ½ pounds **crimini mushrooms**

6 cloves **garlic**, minced

salt and **pepper**

1 cup **white wine**

1 (28-ounce) can **diced tomatoes**, with juice

½ cup **whole black olives**

2 tablespoons minced **fresh basil**

4. Add white wine and diced tomatoes, bring up to a boil, and reduce heat to low. Cover and simmer for 1 hour, stirring occasionally.

5. Add olives and basil, stir, and cook for 5 additional minutes before serving.

HELPFUL TIPS

Add a pinch of crushed red pepper flakes in step 4 for a spicier sauce.

CREAMY CHICKEN THIGH CASSEROLE

prep time **20** mins   cook time **75** mins   serves **8** people   Jan Muller

This creamy chicken thigh casserole is a hit with both adults and kids. You can serve it with roasted potatoes (see my tip at the bottom of the page) or even over egg noodles like a stroganoff.

SHOPPING LIST

8 chicken thighs

1 tablespoon **olive oil**

½ **onion**, diced

1 clove **garlic**, minced

1 pinch **paprika**

1 (**10.75**-ounce) can **cream of chicken soup**

1 (**1**-ounce) packet **onion soup mix**

8 ounces **cream cheese**, cubed

½ cup **chicken broth** or **stock**

1 tablespoon **lemon juice**

⅛ teaspoon **pepper**

1. Preheat oven to 350 degrees.

2. Place oil in a large sauté pan and heat on high.

3. Place chicken in the hot pan, and cook 4 to 5 minutes on each side, until browned. Transfer to a baking dish.

4. Add onion and garlic to the hot pan and sauté until soft. Place over the chicken in the baking dish.

5. In a large mixing bowl, combine all remaining ingredients and microwave on high for about 3 minutes, just until cream cheese is melted and combined. Pour over chicken in the baking dish.

6. Bake chicken for 1 hour and serve hot.

HELPFUL TIPS

For an all-in-one meal, simply add a few potatoes, chopped into cubes, to the baking dish before baking.

CHICKEN LO MEIN

prep time **30** mins · cook time **20** mins · serves **8** people · Jan Muller

Traditionally Lo Mein is not stir-fried, but I find that this preparation is the easiest and most flavorful way to make the Chinese noodle dish at home. Shitake mushrooms are now pretty easy to find in most grocery stores, but you can substitute with any other kind of mushroom in a pinch.

1. Whisk together sugar, rice wine vinegar, soy sauce, sesame oil, and cornstarch to create a marinade. Seal ½ of the marinade with the chicken thighs in a vacuum seal bag, and refrigerate for up to 24 hours. Reserve the remaining marinade.

2. Add olive oil to a large sauté pan and heat on high.

3. Remove chicken from the marinade (discarding marinade) and add it to the hot pan, stir-frying for 6 to 8 minutes. Remove and reserve.

4. Add ginger, garlic, carrots, mushrooms, and scallions to the hot pan, and stir-fry for 2-3 minutes before returning the cooked chicken to the pan.

SHOPPING LIST

8 boneless, skinless chicken thighs, cut into strips

2 tablespoons **sugar**

½ cup **rice wine vinegar**

1 cup **soy sauce**, regular or reduced sodium

2 tablespoons **sesame oil**

¼ cup **cornstarch**

2 tablespoons **olive oil**

3 tablespoons minced **fresh ginger**

2 tablespoons **minced garlic**

1 cup shredded **carrots**

1 pound **shitake mushrooms**, sliced

6 scallions, sliced thinly

3 ½ cups **chicken broth** or **stock**

2 pounds **linguine pasta**, cooked and drained

5. Add the remaining ½ of the marinade created in step 1 and the chicken broth to the pan, bring up to a boil, and reduce heat to low. Simmer for 4-5 minutes, until sauce has thickened.

6. Add cooked linguine to the pan, stir to coat with sauce, and then serve immediately.

HELPFUL TIPS

If you have any leftovers, add more chicken broth and turn it into an Asian chicken noodle soup for lunch the next day.

Orange Chicken Legs with Fingerling Potatoes

ORANGE CHICKEN LEGS WITH FINGERLING POTATOES

prep time **25** mins   cook time **1** hour   serves **4** people   Jan Muller

Oranges go amazingly well with just about any type of meat, but for whatever reason, I absolutely love them with dark chicken meat like the chicken drumsticks in this recipe. Fingerling potatoes are another one of my favorites, but if you have any difficulty finding them, you can always substitute them with red bliss or Yukon gold.

1. Whisk together oil, red pepper flakes, tarragon, salt, pepper, and the zest of the oranges to create a marinade. Seal the marinade and chicken legs in a vacuum seal bag and refrigerate for up to 24 hours.

2. Preheat oven to 425 degrees.

3. Transfer chicken and marinade into a large mixing bowl, and add onions and potatoes. Toss all to coat vegetables, and then drain all excess marinade.

4. Transfer chicken and vegetables to a sheet pan, and bake 15 minutes.

5. Reduce the oven temperature to 375 degrees, and continue baking for 35-45 minutes, basting chicken with the juices from the pan every 15 minutes.

6. Serve garnished with the orange segments.

SHOPPING LIST

8 chicken legs

⅓ cup **olive oil**

½ teaspoon **red pepper flakes**

2 teaspoons minced **fresh tarragon**

¼ teaspoon **salt**

⅛ teaspoon **pepper**

2 oranges, zested and segmented

2 onions, sliced thickly

24 fingerling potatoes, halved lengthwise

HELPFUL TIPS

If using any potatoes larger than fingerling, quarter them before baking to ensure that they are fully cooked by the time the chicken is ready.

Chicken and Dumplings

CHICKEN AND DUMPLINGS

prep time **10** mins | cook time **6-7** hrs | serves **8** people | Bob Warden

Here's a simple and quick preparation for a slow-cooked favorite. The secret to making this so easily is using canned biscuits in place of homemade dumplings—it may sound strange, but they cook into the broth just like a dumpling!

SHOPPING LIST

8 skinless chicken thighs

1 onion, diced

2 (**10.75**-ounce) cans **condensed cream of chicken soup**

3 cups **chicken broth** or **stock**

salt and **pepper**

2 (**10**-ounce) cans **refrigerated biscuits**

1. Place chicken and diced onion into a slow cooker.

2. Whisk together cream of chicken soup and chicken broth, and pour over chicken.

3. Cover slow cooker, and cook on low for 5 to 6 hours. Add salt and pepper to taste.

4. Tear raw biscuit dough into dumpling sized pieces and place them on top of the cooked chicken still in the slow cooker. Cover again, and cook for an additional 45 minutes before serving.

HELPFUL TIPS

You can use boneless chicken thighs or thighs with the bone still in for this recipe—it's up to you. Many people don't like bones in a broth-based dish like this one, but they do add a lot of flavor to the broth as it cooks.

BARBECUED CHICKEN QUESADILLAS

prep time **15** mins   cook time **30** mins   serves **8** people   Bob Warden

P an-fried quesadillas are great, but when I am cooking for a crowd, I defer to the easier oven method that is used for this recipe. Serve with plenty of salsa, sour cream, or guacamole for dipping!

SHOPPING LIST

6 chicken legs, roasted and meat pulled

3 tablespoons **olive oil**

3 **onions**, sliced thinly

2 green bell peppers, sliced thinly

1 cup **barbecue sauce**

2 cups **shredded Mexican cheese blend**

16 (**12** inch) **flour tortillas**

1. Preheat oven to 350 degrees.

2. Add oil to a sauté pan and heat on high.

3. Add onions and peppers to the hot pan, and sauté until soft.

4. Add barbecue sauce and cooked chicken to the hot pan, and sauté until heated through.

5. Lay out 8 flour tortillas on sheet pans, top with ⅛ of the chicken mixture, and spread out evenly. For each tortilla, top the chicken mixture with an equal amount of the Mexican cheese blend, and cover with another flour tortilla.

6. Put sheet pans in the oven and bake for 20 minutes, or until cheese is bubbly hot.

7. Transfer the quesadillas to a cutting board and slice before serving.

HELPFUL TIPS

Lightly spray each tortilla with butter flavored nonstick cooking spray for the buttery goodness of pan-fried quesadillas without all the work of frying each individually.

CHICKEN CURRY

prep time **20** mins　　cook time **35** mins　　serves **6** people　　Jan Muller

When I make this stew-like curry dish the house always smells so good that people come running into the kitchen. Most curry dishes are served over rice, but I like to serve this one over boiled new potatoes.

1. Add oil to a large pot and heat on medium-high.

2. Add onion and garlic to the pot, and sauté until onions are golden brown.

3. Add the cooked chicken, curry powder, ginger, cinnamon, cloves, and cayenne pepper to the pot and stir to distribute spices.

4. Add the diced tomatoes, chicken broth, and coconut milk, and stir to combine.

5. Reduce heat to low and simmer for 20-25 minutes. Salt to taste and stir in the cilantro before serving.

SHOPPING LIST

12 chicken thighs, cooked and meat pulled

2 tablespoons **olive oil**

1 onion, sliced thinly

3 cloves **garlic**, minced

2 tablespoons **curry powder**

1 teaspoon **ground ginger**

¼ teaspoon **cinnamon**

⅛ teaspoon **ground cloves**

⅛ teaspoon **cayenne pepper**

½ (**28**-ounce) can **diced tomatoes**, with juice

3 ½ cups **chicken broth** or **stock**

1 (**13.5**-ounce) can **coconut milk**

salt

2 tablespoons minced **fresh cilantro**

HELPFUL TIPS

While you can chop up the cooked, boneless, skinless chicken thighs to start this dish—removing the meat from the bone after cooking will yield moister meat in the final dish.

Mexican Stuffed Chicken Thighs

MEXICAN STUFFED CHICKEN THIGHS

prep time **20** mins   cook time **20** mins   serves **4** people   Jan Muller

Stuffed chicken takes a little extra effort to make, but the results will impress your guests. Stuffed with only roasted red peppers and cheese and topped with a sauce made from only two ingredients, this recipe packs a ton of flavor from of an inexpensive shopping trip.

1. In a food processor, combine 2 ounces of the roasted red peppers with the sour cream, pulsing until smooth. Reserve.

2. Place oil in a large sauté pan and heat on medium-high.

3. Cut pockets in chicken thighs and season generously with salt and pepper.

4. Stuff pockets with the remaining roasted pepper strips and ¾ of the shredded cheese, and then roll thighs up to hold filling in place.

SHOPPING LIST

8 boneless, skinless chicken thighs

2 (12-ounce) jars **roasted red pepper strips**

1 cup **sour cream**

3 tablespoons **olive oil**

salt and **pepper**

½ cup **shredded Mexican cheese blend**

2 cups **breadcrumbs**

3 tablespoons chopped **fresh cilantro**

2 large eggs, beaten

5. In a large bowl, combine the breadcrumbs and cilantro. Dip stuffed thighs in egg and then in the breadcrumb mixture to coat.

6. Add chicken to the hot pan and sauté for 8 to 10 minutes to brown. Flip chicken, and sauté for another 8 to 10 minutes to brown the other side.

7. Serve immediately, drizzled with the reserved red pepper and sour cream sauce.

HELPFUL TIPS

I like to add fresh spinach to the stuffing as well. Simply sauté the spinach for 2-3 minutes, just until it wilts, and then squeeze the excess liquid out of it with your hands before stuffing.

Dark Meat Chicken Potpie

DARK MEAT CHICKEN POTPIE

prep time **25** mins | cook time **50** mins | serves **8** people | Bob Warden

I grew up eating potpies, which are the perfect, hot, buttery-crusted comfort dish that also provides a healthy dose of vegetables. You simply will not find anything half as good as this version in your grocer's freezer!

SHOPPING LIST

1 pound **chicken thigh meat**, cooked and shredded

2 tablespoons **olive oil**

1 cup diced **carrots**

1 cup diced **celery**

1 **onion**, diced

⅓ cup **all purpose flour**

2 cups **chicken broth** or **stock**

1 cup **frozen peas**

2 tablespoons chopped **fresh tarragon**

salt and **pepper**

2 (**9**-inch) **unbaked pie crusts**

1 large **egg**, beaten

1. Preheat oven to 425 degrees.

2. Place oil in a large sauté pan and heat on high. Add carrots, celery, and onion to the pan and sauté until onions are soft.

3. Stir in flour and cook for 1 minute before adding the cooked chicken. Slowly stir in chicken broth, simmering until thickened.

4. Add peas and tarragon to the pan, and then season with salt and pepper to taste.

5. Meanwhile, line a pie pan with 1 pie crust and then pour the hot filling into it. Cover with the second pie crust, crimping the edges, and brush the top with some of the beaten egg. Pierce holes in the top to vent steam.

6. Place potpie on a sheet pan, and bake 30-35 minutes or until crust is golden brown. Let rest 10 minutes before serving.

HELPFUL TIPS

Add cubed potatoes to make this dish a full meal! You can also save a little time by buying a frozen vegetable medley in place of the carrots, celery, and onion. Simply add them in with the peas in step 4.

CHICKEN NOODLE SOUP

prep time **20** mins   cook time **1** hour   serves **8** people   Bob Warden

There simply is no better soup than this one for raising your temperature on a chilly day! Any combination of vegetables will do, but the ones that I've included in this recipe just so happen to be my favorite combination.

1. Combine olive oil, oregano, thyme, and poultry seasoning to create a marinade. Seal marinade and chicken in a vacuum seal bag, and refrigerate for up to 24 hours.

2. Preheat oven to 375 degrees. Add butter to a stockpot and heat on high.

3. Add onion, carrots, celery, garlic, parsnip, and green beans to the pot and sauté until onions are soft.

4. Meanwhile, remove chicken from the marinade, place on a sheet pan, and bake for 30 minutes.

5. Transfer the baked chicken to the stockpot and cover with the chicken broth. Bring to a boil, reduce the heat to medium-low, and simmer for 30 minutes.

SHOPPING LIST

4 **chicken leg quarters**

2 teaspoons **olive oil**

½ teaspoon **dry oregano**

¼ teaspoon **dry thyme**

¼ teaspoon **poultry seasoning**

2 tablespoons **butter**

1 cup chopped **onion**

1 cup chopped **carrots**

1 cup chopped **celery**

4 cloves **garlic**, minced

1 cup chopped **parsnip**

1 cup trimmed **green beans**

10 cups **chicken broth** or **stock**

2 cups **wide egg noodles**, uncooked

1 cup **heavy cream**

salt and **pepper**

6. Remove chicken from the soup, pull the meat from the bones, and return the meat to the pot.

7. Add noodles, and simmer for 15-20 minutes or until noodles are cooked. Stir in heavy cream and simmer for 10 additional minutes before adding salt and pepper to taste.

HELPFUL TIPS

You can replace the egg noodles in this recipe with any type of pasta, but I really think that wide egg noodles really give a soup that homemade touch.

Chicken Wings

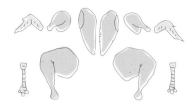

There was a time not so long ago, when chicken wings were used as scraps worthy only of soup or even just making stock for soup. Then the Buffalo sprouted wings. Today, hot Buffalo wings are about as popular as an appetizer can get. This original discovery for using chicken wings inspired chefs to find new preparations and flavorings to prolong America's newfound love affair with the wings of chickens.

Before trying the chicken wing recipes in this section, take a look at how they came to be such a favorite. Our ancestors used all parts of the chicken. Usually the wings, back, and neck were used to flavor soups and stocks, as mentioned above. Commercialization of the poultry market and modern refrigeration methods allowed consumers to begin choosing their favorite cuts of chicken—usually breast, thigh, and leg portions sold well in their own separate packages—with the rest of the bird ending up in soup factories. Chicken wings had fallen out of favor until an enterprising restaurateur came up with a chicken wing recipe that would soon sweep the world off of its feet… or at least into their favorite neighborhood bar.

There is argument over who originated the hot, or Buffalo wing, but most give the honor to the Anchor Bar in Buffalo, New York. One day in 1964, then owner Teresa Bellissimo was faced with feeding her son and his friends a late snack. Having a lot of chicken wings on hand, she fried up the wings, dipped them in butter and chile sauce, and served them with celery and blue cheese dressing to cut the heat. The wings were an almost instant hit and she quickly added them to the Anchor Bar's menu.

While we can't offer you the excitement of trying the world's very first Buffalo wing, we can offer 4 of our favorite chicken wing recipes to try… including the classic with blue cheese.

CONTENTS

Caramelized Chicken Wings

CARAMELIZED CHICKEN WINGS

prep time **15** mins   cook time **25** mins   serves **6** people   Bob Warden

I find this tamarind, honey, and cayenne marinade makes chicken wings fly from the table. Tamarind on its own has a sweet and sour flavor, so it matches nicely with the honey and cayenne. While this sauce is associated with Indian cuisine, I always find it next to the soy sauce in my store's Asian section.

SHOPPING LIST

5 pounds **fresh chicken wings**

4 tablespoons **olive oil**

¼ cup **tamarind sauce**

½ cup **ketchup**

¾ cup **honey**

1 clove **garlic**, minced

¼ teaspoon **cayenne pepper**

salt

1. Whisk together 2 tablespoons of the olive oil, tamarind sauce, ketchup, honey, garlic, and cayenne pepper. Place mixture and chicken wings in a vacuum seal bag and marinate up to 24 hours.

2. Preheat oven to 375 degrees.

3. Add remaining 2 tablespoons of oil to a large, oven safe sauté pan and heat on high.

4. Remove chicken from marinade and place wings in the sauté pan. Cook for 8 to 10 minutes, flip, and cook an additional 8 to 10 minutes.

5. Place pan in oven and bake 5 minutes. Salt to taste before serving.

HELPFUL TIPS

If your super market does not carry tamarind sauce, just substitute with soy sauce and add a little more honey, it's just as nice.

HOT HONEY CHICKEN WINGS

prep time **15** mins　　cook time **20** mins　　serves **10** people　　Bob Warden

SHOPPING LIST

A honey and cayenne combination creates the perfect coating in this backyard dish. However, if you don't have a backyard, no worries, just use the broiler. I separate the wing joints when I am grilling chicken wings just to get better grill marks, but you can skip this step if you are in a hurry.

5 pounds **fresh chicken wings**, separated at joints and tips removed

salt and **pepper**

2 ½ cups **Louisiana hot sauce**

1 cup **ketchup**

¾ cup **butter**

1 cup **honey**

1 teaspoon **cayenne pepper**

1. Lightly oil a grill or indoor grill pan, and then heat on high.

2. Generously season wings with salt and pepper, place chicken wings on grill for 8 to 10 minutes, flip, and grill for 8 to 10 more minutes.

3. Meanwhile, heat the remaining ingredients in a saucepan, whisking to blend, and simmer for 10 minutes.

4. Transfer wings to a bowl, pour sauce over wings, stir to coat, and serve immediately.

HELPFUL TIPS

This recipe is SPICY! Though I make them with the cayenne pepper, you may want to leave it out until you've given the sauce a taste. You can also cut the hot sauce down to only 1 cup for much milder wings.

MUSTARD AND ONION FRIED CHICKEN WINGS

prep time **15** mins   cook time **16** mins   serves **10** people   Jan Muller

I don't always want my chicken wings spicy; I do however, always want them to have lots of flavor. My favorite alternative to spicy Buffalo wings is this 24-hour Dijon and onion marinade. It provides the perfect spark for frying these wings.

SHOPPING LIST

5 pounds **fresh chicken wings**, separated at joint and tips removed

¼ teaspoon **dry thyme**

2 tablespoons **garlic powder**

2 tablespoons **onion powder**

3 tablespoons **Dijon mustard**

vegetable oil for frying

3 cups **all purpose flour**

salt

1. Combine thyme, garlic powder, onion powder, and Dijon mustard to create a marinade. Seal marinade with chicken wings in a vacuum seal bag and refrigerate up to 24 hours.

2. Place 1 inch of oil in a frying pan and heat oil to 350 degrees.

3. Remove chicken wings from marinade and place in flour to coat.

4. Place floured chicken in the hot oil, fry for 6 to 8 minutes, flip, and fry for an additional 6 to 8 minutes.

5. Transfer chicken to some paper towels to drain off excess fat, salt to taste, and serve.

HELPFUL TIPS

For even more mustardy greatness, try serving these wings with honey mustard dressing for dipping.

Classic Chicken Wings with Blue Cheese

CLASSIC CHICKEN WINGS WITH BLUE CHEESE

prep time **15** mins — cook time **15** mins — serves **10** people — Jan Muller

This is my simplest recipe for classic hot wings. There are many hot sauces out on the market, and they vary greatly in their hotness, so be sure to test a couple out to find one you really like. I simply include "Louisiana" hot sauce in this recipe because it is one of the easiest to find and somewhat mild, but with a good bite.

SHOPPING LIST

5 pounds **fresh chicken wings**

½ cup **butter**

⅔ cup **Louisiana hot sauce**

½ teaspoon **garlic powder**

1 cup **all purpose flour**

1 teaspoon **paprika**

½ teaspoon **cayenne pepper**

1 teaspoon **onion powder**

½ teaspoon **salt**

¼ teaspoon **pepper**

carrot and celery sticks, optional

blue cheese dressing

oil for frying

1. Preheat deep fryer to 375 degrees.

2. Place butter, Louisiana hot sauce, and garlic powder in a saucepan and heat on low, whisking to blend.

3. In a bowl, mix together flour, paprika, cayenne pepper, onion powder, salt, and pepper.

4. Toss chicken wings in the flour mixture.

5. Fry chicken wings in the hot oil for 12 to 15 minutes.

6. Transfer chicken from fryer to a bowl, coat with hot sauce mixture, and serve with carrot and celery sticks and blue cheese dressing.

HELPFUL TIPS

If you ever find that your finished wings are too spicy for your taste, the easiest way to "cool" them down is to simply toss them in more melted butter until it thins out the sauce.

WHOLE CHICKEN

Whole roast chicken may be the number one roast served around the world. Whole chickens can be flavored with as little as salt and pepper, and they are always delicious. From there, the possible variety of spices, rubs, herbs, garlic, and onions is endless. When purchased in bulk, whole chickens usually come in 2-packs, with each chicken in a separate vacuum package. As we are writing this, whole chickens purchased this way are still available for under a dollar a pound on a regular basis.

You have the option of butchering these whole chickens for further savings on buying the pieces separately. Though it feels strange writing this, the best way to learn how to efficiently butcher a chicken is to watch a video on the internet. Searching www.google.com for "How to Butcher a Chicken" will lead you to step by step videos that can show the process far better than we could put on a page. It's quick and easy and well worth the time, if maximum savings is your goal. That said, even we are usually quite content with the savings we get on already butchered chicken pieces at warehouse clubs.

A crispy roasted chicken is a thing of beauty. For the best, golden brown roasted chicken, all you have to do is follow these easy steps. First, rub a thin layer of softened butter over the entire outside surface of the chicken. Don't worry about the calories; most of this butter is going to melt off by the time the chicken is done. The butter's job is to help the skin crisp up during the roasting process, and to prevent the skin from drying out as it sheds the layer of fat underneath. Second, start the chicken in a preheated oven at 450 degrees for the first fifteen minutes. Then, turn the oven down to 300 degrees for the remainder of the baking. Always use a meat thermometer to determine when the chicken is done, as chicken is the one dish you never want to under or overcook. When the meat thermometer reaches 190 degrees, the USDA says it is safe to eat… and we say that it is delicious!

CONTENTS

Garlic Chicken

prep time **15** mins   cook time **1 ¾** hrs   serves **6** people   Bob Warden

Although I call this Garlic Chicken, the secret ingredient is actually apple cider! It adds a nice sweetness that pairs well with the roasted garlic. If you happen to have apples in the house, cut them up and put them in the bottom of the pan before roasting to infuse with even more aromatic apple flavor.

Shopping List

1 **whole chicken**, about **3** pounds

¼ cup **butter**, melted

6 cloves **garlic**, minced

1 ½ teaspoons **onion powder**

¼ teaspoon **paprika**

salt and **pepper**

½ cup **chicken broth** or **stock**

½ cup **apple cider**

1. Preheat oven to 350 degrees.

2. Place chicken in a roasting pan, and pour melted butter over top. Sprinkle with the minced garlic, onion powder, paprika, and a generous amount of salt and pepper.

3. Pour chicken broth and apple cider into the bottom of the pan.

4. Bake for 1 hour and 45 minutes, basting occasionally.

5. Let rest 10 minutes before carving. Serve drizzled with juices from the pan.

Helpful Tips

Add a few tablespoons of butter to the pan juices before drizzling over the carved chicken to create a quick and delicious apple and garlic gravy.

Chicken Tortilla Soup

CHICKEN TORTILLA SOUP

prep time **30** mins   cook time **8** hrs   serves **8** people   Bob Warden

Though this recipe has a lengthy (but healthy) list of ingredients, it is so easy to prepare! Just toss it all in a slow cooker and leave it be! It only gets better the longer that it cooks, so put it in before work, and you'll have dinner waiting for you when you get home. Everyone loves a good recipe that makes life easier, especially one that kids love too.

1. Add all ingredients, except for the salt, pepper, and tortilla chips, to a slow cooker.

2. Cover and slow cook on low for 6 to 8 hours.

3. Add salt and pepper to taste before serving topped with the crumbled tortilla chips.

SHOPPING LIST

1 **whole chicken**, cooked, meat pulled

1 (28-ounce) can **diced tomatoes**, with juice

2 **onions**, diced

1 pound **mushrooms**, sliced

2 **green bell peppers**, chopped

2 **jalapeños**, seeded and chopped

1 (16-ounce) package **frozen corn**

2 cloves **garlic**, minced

8 cups **chicken broth or stock**

2 teaspoons **cumin**

2 teaspoons **chili powder**

1 **bay leaf**

2 tablespoons chopped **fresh cilantro**

salt and **pepper**

1 bag **tortilla chips**, crumbled

HELPFUL TIPS

Try garnishing with shredded Cheddar cheese, sour cream, and a dash of fresh lime juice. If you can find them, thin tortilla strips are even better than the crumbled chips. They are usually sold in the organic snack section of the grocery store.

Chicken Fried Rice

CHICKEN FRIED RICE

prep time **25** mins   cook time **15** mins   serves **6** people   Bob Warden

This dish is more than just rice… it's an entire family meal! Making fried rice is a perfect way to use up leftovers, as you can add any vegetables you wish and as little or as much cooked, leftover chicken that you have on hand. When I'm making this from scratch, I like to add a lot of roasted chicken for a very hearty meal that is anything but a side dish!

1. Add the oil to a large sauté pan and heat on high.

2. Add onion, carrots, both bell peppers, and celery to the pan and stir-fry 5 to 6 minutes, or until vegetables begin to soften.

3. Add chicken and snow peas to the pan and stir-fry 3 to 4 more minutes.

4. Add rice, stir-frying until heated throughout.

5. Add scrambled eggs, frozen peas, soy sauce, and sesame oil, and stir-fry until peas are warmed throughout. Serve immediately.

SHOPPING LIST

1 whole chicken, cooked, meat removed and cubed

1 tablespoon **olive oil**

1 onion, diced

2 carrots, diced

1 red bell pepper, diced

1 green bell pepper, diced

2 stalks **celery**, diced

1 cup **snow peas**

6 cups **cooked white rice**

2 large eggs, scrambled

1 cup **frozen peas**

⅓ cup **soy sauce**, regular or reduced sodium

1 ½ teaspoons **sesame oil**

HELPFUL TIPS

After opening frozen vegetables, like the peas in this recipe, I always vacuum seal any that remains before returning them to the freezer to reduce the risk of freezer burn.

SPICY HERB ROASTED CHICKEN

prep time **15** mins   cook time **1** hour   serves **6** people   Jan Muller

This fast, no-fuss recipe is not only flavorful, but SPICY! This recipe is a great cross between a traditional herb roasted chicken and Buffalo wings and has enough meat to feed a family of six! And since you can eat the breast meat with a knife and fork, there's no need to get hot sauce all over your fingers.

1. Preheat oven to 425 degrees.

2. In a small bowl, combine rosemary, oregano, basil, paprika, cayenne pepper, salt, and pepper.

3. In a separate bowl, combine the melted butter and hot sauce.

4. Place chicken in a baking dish and spread melted butter mixture over all surfaces of the skin. Over the butter, coat the chicken with the spice and herb mixture.

5. Bake for 15 minutes. Reduce the heat to 375 degrees, and continue baking for 1 hour and 15 minutes.

6. Let rest for 10 minutes before carving.

SHOPPING LIST

1 whole chicken, about **3 pounds**

1 teaspoon **dry rosemary**

¼ teaspoon **dry oregano**

¼ teaspoon **dry basil**

¼ teaspoon **paprika**

⅛ teaspoon **cayenne pepper**

¼ teaspoon **salt**

⅛ teaspoon **pepper**

3 tablespoons **butter**, melted

¼ cup **hot sauce**

HELPFUL TIPS

For even more flavor, use a meat injector to inject a little of the hot sauce mixture into the meat itself before baking.

BACON AND ONION ROASTED CHICKEN

prep time **30** mins   cook time **1½** hrs   serves **6** people   Jan Muller

Wrapping anything in bacon is a surefire way to add (the best) flavor and moistness! Wrapping a chicken breast in bacon is good—but why not wrap a whole chicken in bacon? This recipe proves that it's not only possible, but delicious!

1. Preheat oven to 425 degrees.

2. Combine softened butter, thyme, paprika, onion, salt, and pepper.

3. Place chicken into a roasting pan, and spread all surfaces of the bird with the butter mixture.

4. Wrap one piece of bacon around each leg and wing, securing with toothpicks. Lay the remaining bacon over top the breast and secure with more toothpicks.

SHOPPING LIST

1 whole chicken, about **3** pounds

2 tablespoons **butter**, softened

1 teaspoon **dry thyme**

½ teaspoon **paprika**

¼ cup minced **onion**

¼ teaspoon **salt**

⅛ teaspoon **pepper**

12 slices **bacon**

1 (10.75-ounce) can **French onion soup**

toothpicks

5. Pour French onion soup in bottom of the pan, place in oven, and bake for 15 minutes.

6. Reduce the heat to 375 degrees, and continue baking for 1 hour and 15 minutes. Let rest for 15 minutes before removing toothpicks and carving.

HELPFUL TIPS

The easiest way to serve this is to remove the bacon slices before carving the chicken. Simply crumble the bacon, and serve the carved meat topped with a handful of the crumbles.

Tuscan Chicken

TUSCAN CHICKEN

prep time **15** mins   cook time **1 ¾** hrs   serves **6** people   Jan Muller

This simple roasted chicken is a quick and easy to prep family meal that is also hearty and delicious. Add a few fingerling potatoes to the roasting pan and you've got the entire dinner covered. My secret ingredient here is a little bit of ground mustard, which adds a nice bite that you won't find in most family-style roasted chickens.

1. Preheat oven to 350 degrees.

2. Place onions, zucchini, and celery in a roasting pan, and then place chicken over top.

3. In a bowl, whisk together lemon juice, zest, and olive oil, and drizzle over chicken and vegetables.

4. Combine Italian seasoning, ground mustard, minced garlic, salt, and pepper, and sprinkle over top chicken and vegetables.

SHOPPING LIST

1 whole chicken, about **3** pounds

2 onions, sliced thinly

4 zucchini, cut into ½ inch wedges

6 stalks **celery**, cut into ½ inch lengths

4 lemons, juiced and zested

¼ cup **olive oil**

1 tablespoon **Italian seasoning**

½ teaspoon **ground mustard**

2 teaspoons **minced garlic**

½ teaspoon **salt**

¼ teaspoon **pepper**

5. Bake for 1 hour and 45 minutes, basting occasionally.

6. Remove from oven and let rest for 10 minutes before carving. Serve with vegetables and juices from the pan.

HELPFUL TIPS

Adding ¼ cup of white wine to the lemon juice, zest, and olive oil will give this recipe a gourmet French flavor, even though the rest of the recipe is Italian!

Southern Fried Chicken

SOUTHERN FRIED CHICKEN

prep time **15** mins   cook time **24** mins   serves **6** people   Bob Warden

Summers on my great grandmother's farm are still vivid in my memory. I helped with whisking and dipping for this crisp and golden fried chicken that is now a regular feature on my own table. I hope you and your family make this dish together too, creating your own memories!

SHOPPING LIST

1 **whole chicken**, cut into pieces

1 quart **vegetable oil**

2 cups **all purpose flour**

2 teaspoons **dry thyme**

2 teaspoons **ground mustard**

2 teaspoons **paprika**

½ teaspoon **salt**

¼ teaspoon **pepper**

3 **large eggs**

1 cup **buttermilk**

1. Add vegetable oil to a large frying pan and heat to 350 degrees.

2. In a large bowl, combine flour, thyme, ground mustard, paprika, salt, and pepper.

3. In another bowl, whisk together eggs and buttermilk.

4. Double-bread the chicken pieces by dipping them into the buttermilk mixture, then into flour, then back into the buttermilk mixture, and back into the flour.

5. Place coated chicken in the hot oil and fry 10 to 12 minutes. Flip pieces, and fry another 10 to 12 minutes, until golden brown.

6. Drain on paper towels to remove excess grease, and serve.

HELPFUL TIPS

Vacuum sealing the chicken pieces in the egg and buttermilk mixture and refrigerating overnight before breading will make your fried chicken even more moist and delicious!

SLOW COOKER CHICKEN

prep time **30** mins cook time **6-8** hrs serves **6** people Bob Warden

This recipe is perfect for putting into the slow cooker in the morning for a fall-off-the-bone dinner in the evening. The best part is that, after dinner, you are left with a really great base for a soup in the slow cooker. Just cut up any leftover meat, add it back to the slow cooker with more broth and some dry pasta, and you'll have a wonderful chicken noodle soup.

SHOPPING LIST

1 whole chicken, about **3** pounds

2 teaspoons **paprika**

½ teaspoon **cayenne pepper**

1 teaspoon **onion powder**

1 teaspoon **garlic powder**

1 teaspoon **dry thyme**

salt and **pepper**

1 onion, sliced thickly

4 stalks **celery**, sliced thickly

1 carrot, sliced thickly

2 cups **chicken broth** or **stock**

1. Sprinkle chicken with paprika, cayenne pepper, onion powder, garlic powder, thyme, and a generous amount of salt and pepper.

2. Place into a vacuum seal bag, seal, and refrigerate for up to 24 hours.

3. Remove chicken from the vacuum seal bag and place into a slow cooker. Surround with the onion, celery, and carrot, and pour broth over top.

4. Slow cook on low for 6-8 hours before carving and serving alongside the vegetables.

HELPFUL TIPS

After slow cooking, heat for a few minutes under the broiler to dry out and crisp up the skin before serving.

Asian Chicken with Peanuts

prep time **10** mins   cook time **1** hour   serves **6** people   Jan Muller

After having a nice chicken and peanut dish at a local Chinese restaurant, I decided to try to make it myself. Instead of using strips of chicken, I opted for whole pieces of chicken so that I could feed a lot for less money. With only a few minutes of prep time, it's not only a money-saver, but a timesaver too!

1. Whisk together chicken broth, soy sauce, sugar, garlic, ginger, cornstarch, and pepper to create a marinade. Seal marinade and chicken pieces in a vacuum seal bag, and refrigerate for up to 24 hours.

2. Preheat oven to 425 degrees.

3. Remove chicken from marinade and place in a baking dish. Bake for 50-55 minutes.

4. Meanwhile, pour marinade into a saucepan over high heat and bring to a boil. Reduce heat to low and simmer until thickened.

5. Add bell pepper, scallions, and cilantro to the saucepan, and simmer for 5 minutes.

Shopping List

1 **whole chicken**, cut into pieces

1 ½ cups **chicken broth or stock**

1 tablespoon **soy sauce**, regular or reduced sodium

1 tablespoon **sugar**

2 cloves **garlic**, minced

1 teaspoon minced **fresh ginger**

1 tablespoon **cornstarch**

⅛ teaspoon **pepper**

1 **red bell pepper**, diced

3 **scallions**, chopped

2 tablespoons minced **fresh cilantro**

1 cup **dry roasted peanuts**

6. Pour sauce over baked chicken, and bake an additional 5 minutes before serving garnished with plenty of the dry roasted peanuts.

Helpful Tips

Serve over steamed white rice to inexpensively stretch this meal even further. For fun, you can buy peanuts in the shell and have the kids shell them while you prepare the chicken.

Honey of a Thyme Roasted Chicken

HONEY OF A THYME ROASTED CHICKEN

prep time **20** mins cook time **1½** hrs serves **6** people Jan Muller

This has been a favorite of mine since I learned from my grandmother that a continuous coating of red wine vinegar and honey makes for a beautifully bronzed (and delicious!) chicken. You can use any fresh herbs in place of the thyme, or a combination of different herbs for even more flavor.

SHOPPING LIST

1 whole chicken, about **3 pounds**

½ cup **red wine vinegar**

½ cup **olive oil**

¼ cup **fresh thyme**

2 tablespoons honey

4 stalks celery, cut into ½ inch lengths

1 onion, sliced thinly

salt and **pepper**

1. Preheat oven to 425 degrees.

2. Whisk together the red wine vinegar, olive oil, thyme, and honey.

3. Place celery and onion in a roasting pan and top with the chicken. Pour the honey mixture over the chicken, letting it drip down into the vegetables. Generously season chicken and vegetables with salt and pepper.

4. Bake for 15 minutes. Reduce the heat to 375 degrees, and continue baking for 1 hour and 15 minutes, basting occasionally.

5. Let rest 10 minutes before carving. Serve with the vegetables and juices from the pan.

HELPFUL TIPS

If you feel the sauce is too strong, simply whisk in a little more honey to mellow it out, but remember that cooking the vinegar really brings out a natural sweetness.

GROUND TURKEY

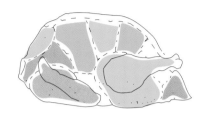

Ground turkey is a wonderful, healthier substitute for ground beef. But wait! Not all ground turkey is equal. Here are the facts… Low fat ground turkey is almost always ground from turkey breast and has around 120 calories per serving, including 10 calories from fat. Often the label says 93/7, which indicates that it is only comprised of 7 percent fat. This is definitely a low calorie option, but you are going to have to do a little work on this ground turkey breast to make sure that it is not only flavorful, but moist, to make it a truly suitable replacement for ground beef. The easiest way to add moisture to ground turkey breast is to add in chopped water filled vegetables, such as zucchini or bell pepper.

Most ground turkey offered in bulk is ground from dark and light meat turkey, and has around 230 calories per serving, including 150 from fat. This calorie and fat content is actually quite close to that of ground beef. Usually labeled as 85/15, this ground turkey is darn good— nearly as tasty as actual ground beef—and can be substituted freely in any ground beef recipes. However, it must be repeated that you are not exactly enjoying a truly low calorie option.

Of course, this is a book about savings, so we can tell you that this richer ground turkey usually costs about 10% less than ground beef. So there you have it.

A rule of thumb: If you are using ground turkey in chili, spaghetti sauce or other dishes where the ground turkey is not standing alone,

or is in a heavy sauce, you can use the leaner ground turkey breast. Most likely, no one will ever notice the difference. However, if you are making a plain turkey burger, we would choose the regular ground turkey with dark meat every time.

In this category, you will find 4 recipes that may inspire you to try substituting ground turkey in some of your favorite ground beef recipes. Whether you choose the ground turkey breast for health, or the regular ground turkey for savings, that is completely up to you.

CONTENTS

SPICY TURKEY BURGERS

prep time **20** mins   cook time **12** mins   serves **6** people   Jan Muller

SHOPPING LIST

For me, ground turkey has less flavor than than ground beef, so I decided to jazz it up and here is the result. I like to make these burgers ahead, vacuum seal and freeze them. If you form the burgers only ½ of an inch thick you can cook them from frozen by adding just 5 minutes to the cook time.

1 ½ pounds **ground turkey**

1 large **egg**

3 tablespoons diced **red bell pepper**

3 tablespoons minced **onion**

¼ cup **soy sauce**, regular or reduced sodium

2 tablespoons **Worcestershire sauce**

2 teaspoons **cumin**

1 teaspoon **ground mustard**

1 teaspoon **paprika**

½ teaspoon **chili powder**

¼ cup **breadcrumbs**

¼ teaspoon **pepper**

1. Lightly oil or spray a grill or indoor grill pan and then heat on medium-high.

2. In a large bowl, combine all ingredients and mix well.

3. Form turkey mixture into 6 equal burger patties.

4. Place burgers on grill, grill 4 to 6 minutes, flip burgers, grill for another 4 to 6 minutes. Serve as you would ordinarily serve burgers, on buns with fixings.

HELPFUL TIPS

Since grilling turkey burgers can dry them out rather quickly, I brush mine with an oil and water mixture after I flip them, just before taking them off the grill.

Ground Turkey and Rice Stuffed Bell Peppers

GROUND TURKEY AND RICE STUFFED BELL PEPPERS

prep time **30** mins   cook time **60** mins   serves **6** people   Bob Warden

My mother always made stuffed peppers with raw rice and it was always hard. I use cooked rice to avoid crunchy uncooked rice and mushy peppers. I like to use an assortment of pepper colors; it looks so pretty coming out of the oven.

1. Preheat oven to 350 degrees.

2. Slice tops off peppers and scrape out seeds. Reserve tops.

3. In a large bowl, combine all other ingredients except marinara sauce. Pack mixture into peppers until overflowing and then cover with the reserved pepper tops.

4. Place stuffed peppers in a large baking dish and then pour ½ cup of water into the bottom of the dish. Cover with aluminum foil and bake 55 to 60 minutes.

SHOPPING LIST

1 ½ pounds **ground turkey**

6 **medium bell peppers**

2 **large eggs**

1 **bell pepper**, diced

2 **large onions**, diced

2 **large tomatoes**, diced

6 cups **cooked rice**

2 tablespoons minced **fresh parsley**

½ teaspoon **salt**

¼ teaspoon **pepper**

2 cups **marinara sauce**

5. Meanwhile, place marinara sauce in a saucepot over medium heat and bring up to a simmer.

6. Serve baked peppers smothered in hot marinara sauce.

HELPFUL TIPS

Prepare a large pot of your own fresh marinara sauce and vacuum seal into multiple portions for making meals exactly like this one. Simply boil the entire bag right out of the freezer to reheat.

Turkey Chili

Turkey Chili

prep time **10** mins · cook time **40** mins · serves **6** people · Jan Muller

I am always searching for different ways to make chili. Sautéing the spices with the turkey really increases the flavor. I usually serve my chili with shredded cheese and sour cream. Serve with crackers, over rice, or even spaghetti!

1. Heat vegetable oil in a large skillet over medium-high heat.

2. Add turkey, onions, and peppers, and sauté until turkey is browned.

3. Add chili powder, garlic, oregano, cumin, paprika, and cayenne pepper and cook 2 minutes, stirring constantly.

4. Add kidney beans and diced tomatoes, bring up to a simmer, and reduce heat to medium-low. Cover and simmer 30 minutes.

5. Add salt and pepper to taste and serve.

Shopping List

1 ¼ pounds **ground turkey**

2 tablespoons **vegetable oil**

1 onion, diced

1 yellow bell pepper, diced

3 tablespoons **chili powder**

1 teaspoon **granulated garlic**

1 teaspoon **dry oregano**

1 teaspoon **cumin**

1 teaspoon **paprika**

1 teaspoon **cayenne pepper**

1 (**16**-ounce) can **red kidney beans**

1 (**28**-ounce) can **diced tomatoes**, with juice

salt and **pepper**

Helpful Tips

If you have a hectic work week, a great idea is to choose one day a week to prepare and vacuum seal several meals in advance. The great thing about chili is that you can literally drop the entire, sealed bag into a pot of boiling water to reheat.

Turkey Burrito Lasagna Casserole

prep time **20** mins · cook time **50** mins · serves **8-10** people · Jan Muller

Lasagna is one of my favorite meals -- I love the layers! One day while eating a burrito I got the idea for this dish and a new lasagna was born. I serve mine with salsa, guacamole, and a bottle of hot sauce.

1. Preheat oven to 350 degrees.

2. Add vegetable oil and ground turkey to a large skillet over high heat, cooking until turkey is well browned. Drain off any excess grease and stir in taco seasoning.

3. In a mixing bowl, combine sour cream and Cheddar cheese soup.

4. Spread ½ of the refried beans across the bottom of a 9x13 casserole dish and then spread ½ sour cream mixture over top of beans.

Shopping List

1 pound **ground turkey**

1 tablespoon **vegetable oil**

1 (1 ¼-ounce) packet **taco seasoning**

4 ounces **sour cream**

1 (10 ¾-ounce) can **Cheddar cheese soup**

1 (16-ounce) can **refried beans**

1 (10-ounce) can **diced tomatoes with green chilies**

3 cups **shredded Mexican cheese blend**

6 large flour tortillas

5. Sprinkle ½ of the ground turkey over top sour cream mixture and then top that with ½ of the diced tomatoes.

6. Sprinkle ⅓ of the shredded Mexican cheese over top tomatoes and then cover all with 3 flour tortillas.

7. Repeat steps 4-6 to create a second layer and then top with the remaining shredded cheese. Bake uncovered for 30-40 minutes. Let rest 15 minutes before slicing into 8-10 slices.

Helpful Tips

After the first 20 minutes of baking, keep an eye on things. If the cheese is browning too much for your liking, simply cover with aluminum foil for the remaining time in the oven.

BABY BACK RIBS

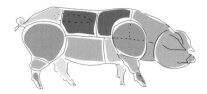

There is no need to worry; baby back ribs are not from baby pigs. They are only named 'baby' in reference to their small size. They are called 'back' because they are located on the backbone. With 13 rib sections, a full slab can be anywhere from 18 to 24 inches long. With their built in handle (the bone), baby back ribs are the quintessential finger-food for any barbecue.

Spareribs, also available in bulk, can be substituted for baby back ribs in most recipes (with a few tweaks). Spareribs are cut from the larger bones along the belly of the pig and contain more meat between the bones, but more fat as well. Spareribs are also acceptable as finger food; you just need bigger, or more, fingers to hold them. Spareribs take about twice the cooking time of baby back ribs, so adjust any recipes accordingly. Though the cooking times are longer, they are usually about half the price of baby back ribs, so they are definitely something to consider.

Par-cooking ribs (or pre-cooking) before you grill them can help reduce the grilling time, which will then reduce the likelihood of them being over-charred by the grill. Simply boil baby back ribs 5 minutes, or spareribs for 10 minutes, to reduce grilling time by as much as half. Or you can use Bob's favorite way to par-cook—a pressure cooker. Simply set to high, and cook under pressure for 5 minutes. We guarantee your guests will ask how you made such super moist ribs without burning them!

Bulk packaged ribs usually come with three or more slabs per package. If you do not need three slabs for your next barbecue, open the package and repack one slab at a time. If you are using a recipe that calls for a marinade, go ahead and add the marinade to the vacuum pack, then refrigerate for up to five days, or freeze for up to six months.

CONTENTS

Chipotle Rockin' Ribs, **155**

Honey Dry Rubbed Ribs, **156**

Old Kentucky Hill Ribs, **157**

Chipotle Rockin' Ribs

CHIPOTLE ROCKIN' RIBS

prep time **10** mins · cook time **3+** hrs · serves **4-6** people · Jan and Bob · p o r k

Like your ribs spicy? Welcome to my Chipotle Rockin' Ribs recipe! I always have plenty of beverages on hand to cool things down, but you can always cut back on the chipotle chilies if you like things a little more mild.

SHOPPING LIST

2 (**2** pound) racks **baby back ribs**

1 ½ cups **ketchup**

1 ½ cups **barbecue sauce**

2 cans (**7** ounces each) **chipotle chilies in adobo sauce**, minced

nonstick cooking spray

3 tablespoons **cornstarch**

1. Place oven rack at the highest position and preheat broiler.

2. Cut ribs into portions of two ribs each. Place ribs on broiler pan and place under broiler for 5 to 7 minutes. Flip ribs, and broil for another 5 to 7 minutes. Remove from oven and turn oven down to 275 degrees.

3. Whisk together ketchup, barbecue sauce, and chipotle chilies to create the sauce, and pour over ribs. Spray a sheet of aluminum foil with nonstick cooking spray and use it to cover ribs. Return to the oven and cook for 3 to 3 ½ hours.

4. Whisk cornstarch into 3 tablespoons of tap water.

5. Pour sauce from rib pan into a saucepan, bring to a boil, and whisk in cornstarch and water mixture, cooking until thickened.

6. Serve immediately, pouring sauce over ribs.

HELPFUL TIPS

The type of barbecue sauce you choose will obviously have a huge impact on the final flavor of this dish. I like to buy a mesquite flavored sauce for this recipe, as the smokiness only adds to the smoky flavor of chipotles.

HONEY DRY RUBBED RIBS

prep time **10** mins   cook time **1-2** hrs   serves **4-6** people   Bob Warden

I've found that by adding cumin and coriander to ribs you give otherwise ordinary ribs an interesting Eastern flair. You can cook up several racks of these in one day, remove the foil, vacuum seal, and freeze. If you let them thaw in the refrigerator, you can quickly grill or bake them just until they are hot throughout.

1. Preheat oven to 350 degrees.

2. In a mixing bowl, combine honey, paprika, chili powder, granulated garlic, cumin, coriander, onion powder, brown sugar, and minced garlic to create a honey rub.

3. Brush ribs with barbecue sauce.

4. Cover barbecue brushed ribs with the honey rub.

5. Wrap each rack in aluminum foil, transfer to a sheet pan, and bake for 1 ½ to 2 hours.

6. Remove from oven, unwrap, and serve immediately.

SHOPPING LIST

2 (2 pound) racks **baby back ribs**

1 ½ cups **honey**

2 teaspoons **paprika**

2 teaspoons **chili powder**

1 teaspoon **granulated garlic**

½ teaspoon **ground cumin**

½ teaspoon **ground coriander**

1 teaspoon **onion powder**

¾ cup **light brown sugar**

1 **onion**, minced

2 cloves **garlic**, minced

1 ½ cups **barbecue sauce**

HELPFUL TIPS

For extra flavor, toast your cumin and coriander on the stove for 3 minutes prior to making the rub.

OLD KENTUCKY HILL RIBS

prep time **20** mins cook time **2+** hrs serves **4-6** people Jan Muller

pork

The whiskey and molasses add a nice underlying sweetness to these ribs, but if you have kids, try replacing the whiskey with cola or root beer for a different, but still unique taste. I do not use molasses often, and somehow it manages to get all over my cabinets when I do. As a solution, I now vacuum seal it before I put it away.

1. Preheat oven to 300 degrees.

2. Generously season ribs with salt and pepper, and then sprinkle with red pepper flakes. Place ¼ cup of tap water and the seasoned ribs in a sheet pan. Cover all with aluminum foil and bake for 2 ½ to 3 hours.

3. Heat olive oil in a sauce pot over high heat and add onion. Sauté until lightly caramelized, reduce heat to low, and add all remaining ingredients. Simmer on low for 30 minutes.

4. Set grill or grill pan to high.

5. Transfer ribs to the hot grill, bone side up, and cook 3-5 minutes on each side, basting the meaty side of ribs with the sauce from the saucepot in the last minute of grilling.

6. Serve immediately, drizzled with any remaining sauce.

SHOPPING LIST

2 (**2** pound) racks **baby back ribs**

salt and **pepper**

1 tablespoon **red pepper flakes**

2 tablespoons **olive oil**

½ cup minced **onion**

1 tablespoon **chili powder**

2 cups **barbecue sauce**

2 teaspoons **whiskey**

1 teaspoon **granulated garlic**

½ teaspoon **onion powder**

2 tablespoons **molasses**

HELPFUL TIPS

Move the ribs to a cooler section of the grill before adding sauce to keep the sugars in the sauce from charring too quickly.

PORK SHOULDER

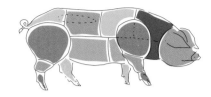

Pork Shoulder is, in our opinion, the most versatile of all the pork cuts. You can even grind shoulder into ground pork for use in meat sauces, meatballs, and homemade sausage patties or links. Because pork shoulder has the perfect ratio of fat to lean meat, it is ideal for both large and small roasts. A pork shoulder roast will be juicy, tender, and very tasty. Also, pork, like chicken, is fairly neutral in flavor, so it adapts well to a multiplicity of flavors, which is perfect for braising and slow cooking. From our travels, we know that this is the reason that pork shoulder is a favorite of Chinese and Mexican chefs… especially when a recipe calls for long, slow cooking. Mu shu pork, sweet and sour pork, pork fried rice, carnitas, fajitas, enchiladas, and quesadillas are all among pork shoulder's greatest achievements. Of course, we can't forget that pork shoulder is most often used for America's favorite slow cooked pork dish—pulled pork—and the pulled pork sandwich! Zowie!

The really good news is that, next to whole chicken, pork shoulder is usually the least expensive cut of meat at your local warehouse club. When you get a gigantic, 11-15 pound pork shoulder home, be prepared to cut several roasts. If you have a meat grinder, take the ends and scraps and grind them into ground pork for sausage or meat sauces. Or combine some of the ground pork with ground beef in many of the ground beef recipes in this book—the combination is delicious!

Do not let the massive size of a bulk pork shoulder scare you off! Pound for pound, it is simply too good of a deal to pass up. Set a plan of action and divide and conquer that piece of meat; dividing, vacuum sealing, and freezing meal-ready roast after roast. You may just want to set aside two of those roasts for two nights of the Pulled Pork recipe in this category… it's that good!

CONTENTS

HUNTER'S STEW

prep time **20** mins cook time **1 ½** hrs serves **10** people Bob Warden

While I am not a hunter, I do love a good stew. I like a lot of cabbage in this, so I use both regular cabbage and pickled sauerkraut for a little extra bite. The really good thing about this dish is that you can turn any leftover stew into an entire pot of Hunter's "Soup" the next day just by adding more beef broth.

1. Place pork, bacon, and kielbasa into a large pot over high heat. Cook until all are browned.

2. Add carrot, onions, garlic, and bay leaves. Cook for 5 minutes, or until onions soften.

3. Add sauerkraut, beef broth, diced tomatoes, basil, marjoram, and mushrooms to the pot. Reduce heat to low, cover, and simmer for 1 hour, stirring occasionally.

4. Meanwhile, bring 4 cups of water and a pinch of salt to a boil in a separate pot. Add cabbage and cook 2 minutes. Drain and reserve cabbage.

5. Combine flour with 2 tablespoons of water. Stir mixture into stew and bring to a boil. Stir in cooked cabbage and cook 3-4 minutes longer. Add salt and pepper to taste and serve immediately.

SHOPPING LIST

1 pound **pork shoulder**, cubed

12 slices **bacon**, diced

1 pound **kielbasa**, cut into ½ inch pieces

1 **carrot**, diced

2 **onions**, diced

3 cloves **garlic**, minced

2 **bay leaves**

1 pound **sauerkraut**

1 cup **beef broth** or **stock**

1 cup diced **tomatoes**

1 teaspoon **dry basil**

1 teaspoon **dry marjoram**

1 cup sliced **mushrooms**

4 cups shredded **green cabbage**

2 tablespoons **all purpose flour**

salt and **pepper**

HELPFUL TIPS

This dish is really good from a slow cooker as well. Simply transfer everything to a slow cooker in step 3 and cook on low for 5-6 hours or until you are ready to eat. Then turn it up to high and finish the recipe as written.

Sweet and Sour Pork

SWEET AND SOUR PORK

prep time **30** mins   cook time **30** mins   serves **8** people   Jan Muller

I prefer to lightly flour my pork for this dish to reduce the fat that the traditional tempura batter of sweet and sour pork can soak up. Jasmine or basmati rice goes nicely with this dish.

1. Whisk sugar, soy sauce, egg whites, and scallions until well combined. Vacuum seal with pork for up to 24 hours to marinate.

2. Add vegetable oil to a large sauté pan or wok over high heat.

3. Remove pork from the marinade, coat with flour, and slowly add to the hot oil in pan. Cook pork until all sides are well browned and meat is cooked throughout. Remove from pan.

4. Drain all but 2 tablespoons of oil from the pan, reduce heat to medium, and add celery, bell peppers, and onions, cooking until soft. Carefully pour 2 cups of tap water into the pan.

5. Create the sauce by adding the sugar, cider vinegar, ketchup, soy sauce, and pineapple chunks to the pan and bringing up to a boil, stirring constantly.

6. Whisk cornstarch into an additional ½ cup of tap water, and stir into the pan, simmering until the sauce is thick. Return fried pork to the vegetables and sauce in pan, stir to evenly coat, and serve immediately.

SHOPPING LIST

2 pounds **pork shoulder**, cut into large cubes

½ teaspoon **sugar**

2 teaspoons **soy sauce**, regular or reduced sodium

2 large egg whites

4 scallions, chopped

1 cup **vegetable oil**

1 cup **all purpose flour**

6 stalks **celery**, cut into **1** inch pieces

2 green bell peppers, julienned

2 onions, chopped

SAUCE

1 ½ cups **sugar**

⅔ cup **cider vinegar**

½ cup **ketchup**

2 teaspoons **soy sauce**, regular or reduced sodium

2 (8-ounce) cans **pineapple chunks**

¼ cup **cornstarch**

HELPFUL TIPS

When you plan to make this recipe, get a large pork shoulder, cube it all up, and vacuum seal and freeze what you do not need for this recipe. That way you are ahead of the game for when you go to make this one again, and I know you will.

Soda Pop Pulled Pork

SODA POP PULLED PORK

prep time **10** mins · cook time **9+** hrs · serves **8** people · Bob Warden

Pulled pork is one of those great barbecue dishes that you simply have to cook all day (unless you own a pressure cooker!), but the time you put in is always worth it in the end. While this recipe does take all day, it's in a slow cooker, so you're free to leave it be.

SHOPPING LIST

1 pork shoulder roast, about **4** pounds

3 cups **birch beer** (may use root beer)

2 (**18**-ounce) bottles **barbecue sauce**

salt and **pepper**

1. Place pork shoulder and birch beer in a slow cooker, and cook on low for 8-10 hours, or until the meat is fork tender.

2. Remove pork shoulder from slow cooker and discard liquid. Pull apart pork and then return pulled pork to slow cooker.

3. Stir in barbecue sauce, and cook another hour on high.

4. Add salt and pepper to taste and serve immediately.

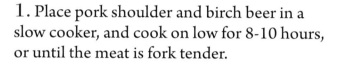

HELPFUL TIPS

For easy pulling of the pork, put cooked chunks of the pork shoulder in a stand mixer and set it to low. Just watch it very closely, as it will pull the pork and then eventually turn it into mush if you aren't paying attention!

ROAST PORK SHOULDER WITH POMEGRANATE SAUCE AND WALNUTS

prep time **10** mins   cook time **3** hrs   serves **6** people   Jan Muller

I use pomegranate juice to put a new twist on a simple pork roast. This way I can reap the added natural health benefits of pomegranate juice, and feel really good about eating way too much of this pork!

SHOPPING LIST

1 **pork shoulder roast**, about **4** pounds

salt and **pepper**

2 teaspoons **minced garlic**

1 ¼ cups **pomegranate juice**

3 tablespoons **balsamic vinegar**

3 tablespoons **light brown sugar**

1 **cinnamon stick**

¼ cup **walnuts**, finely chopped

1. Preheat oven to 325 degrees. Place roast in roasting pan, generously season with salt and pepper, and sprinkle with garlic. Bake for 1 ½ hours.

2. Meanwhile, in a saucepan over medium-high heat, boil the pomegranate juice until liquid has reduced by about half.

3. Remove the pomegranate juice from the heat, and add the balsamic vinegar, brown sugar, and cinnamon stick.

4. Bake roast for another 1 ½ hours, this time basting with the pomegranate sauce every 20 minutes. Sprinkle the roast with the walnuts in the last 20 minutes of baking.

5. Let rest 10 minutes before slicing. Serve smothered in the juices from the pan.

HELPFUL TIPS

Make extra sauce and use as a marinade for pork chops; just vacuum seal together for anywhere from 2 to 24 hours.

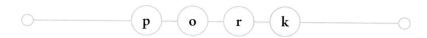

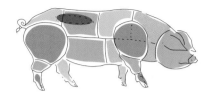

PORK TENDERLOIN

Pork tenderloins are located on the inside of the rib bones, on the sirloin end of the pork loin. The pork tenderloin is by far the most tender cut of pork, even more tender than beef tenderloin. Many chefs use the word 'buttery' to describe its soft, tender, mouth feel. Pork tenderloin is very versatile and can be trimmed and cut into medallions to sauté, or left whole to roast or grill.

Most bulk packages of pork tenderloins come already in a vacuum pack of 2-3 tenderloins, each weighing about 2 pounds.

Pork tenderloins are also perfect for pounding out thin, then breading for a variety of sautéed and fried recipes. Breading can be done in advance, and the breaded pieces separated with wax paper before vacuum sealing for storage. Growing up in Iowa, the pounded pork tenderloin sandwich was a must carry in almost every restaurant. Bob went back last year and the first thing he did was stop at his favorite sandwich shop to order two deep fried, pork tenderloin sandwiches. But don't laugh! That sandwich shop has been around for over 75 years, and the pork tenderloin sandwich is its signature dish.

In this category, Bob tries to recreate his favorite Crispy Iowa Pork Sandwich, and it is most definitely a sandwich that is not to be missed.

Like all pork cuts, the tenderloin is happy to take on the bold flavors of spices, sauces, and marinades. Pork especially pairs well with most fruit. In fact, you can simply roast or grill a pork tenderloin, slice it into medallions, and serve it with a variety of jams and jellies for a simple and delicious meal.

A key to roasting or grilling whole pork tenderloins is to never let them cook past an internal temperature of 150 degrees. Use an instant-read thermometer to monitor the temperature from time to time. Most modern pork has had much of the fat bred out of it, so don't overcook a tenderloin; the minute it reaches proper temperature pull it from the heat and let it rest at room temperature for at least 5 minutes to lock in the juices.

CONTENTS

Spice Rubbed Pork Tenderloin with Apricot Barbecue Glaze

SPICE RUBBED PORK TENDERLOIN WITH APRICOT BARBECUE GLAZE

prep time **20** mins   cook time **25** mins   serves **8** people   Bob Warden

Apricots go wonderfully with grilled meat, especially the pork tenderloin in this recipe. For an even better presentation, buy a few fresh apricots, cut them in half, and pit them, and then grill for a minute or two to serve alongside the pork.

1. Combine all dry rub ingredients and rub into pork tenderloins. Vacuum seal and refrigerate for up to 24 hours.

2. Heat apricot preserves in a saucepan over medium heat until melted. Add remaining glaze ingredients, stir, and remove from heat.

3. Split glaze into two portions, one to brush onto pork, the other to serve alongside the pork.

4. Lightly oil or spray a grill or indoor grill pan, and then heat on high.

5. Place pork tenderloins on the grill for 8 to 10 minutes. Flip, and grill for 6 to 8 additional minutes before brushing with the first portion of the glaze. Grill 2 more minutes.

6. Remove from grill, let rest 5 minutes, slice, and serve alongside remaining glaze.

SHOPPING LIST

2 (**1 pound**) **pork tenderloins**

DRY RUB

1 tablespoon **chili powder**

1 tablespoon **granulated garlic**

½ tablespoon **light brown sugar**

½ teaspoon **salt**

¼ teaspoon **pepper**

GLAZE

1 ½ cups **apricot preserves**

½ cup **barbecue sauce**

¼ teaspoon **ground ginger**

½ teaspoon **granulated garlic**

½ teaspoon **hot sauce**

1 tablespoon chopped **fresh cilantro**

1 **lime**, juiced and zested

HELPFUL TIPS

You can also make this recipe in the oven, baking for 1 hour and 15 minutes at 325 degrees. Simply baste with the glaze in the last 15 minutes of baking.

p
o
r
k

MAPLE GLAZED PORK TENDERLOIN

prep time **15** mins   cook time **12** mins   serves **4** people   Jan and Bob

SHOPPING LIST

2 (**1 pound**) **pork tenderloins**, cut into ½ inch medallions

4 teaspoons **dry thyme**

4 teaspoons **dry marjoram**

1 teaspoon **onion flakes**

2 teaspoons **granulated garlic**

½ teaspoon **salt**

¼ teaspoon **pepper**

2 tablespoons **butter**

¼ cup **maple syrup**

As a kid growing up, I always liked to dip pork sausage in the maple syrup when my mom served pancakes. This recipe is kind of like a grown-up version of that, only minus the pancakes. Serve with hearty chunks of salted, roasted potatoes for another nice contrast to the sweet syrup.

1. Combine thyme, marjoram, onion flakes, garlic, salt, and pepper to create a rub. Rub mixture onto pork medallions and vacuum seal, refrigerating for up to 24 hours.

2. Add butter to a large sauté pan and heat on medium-high.

3. Remove pork from vacuum seal bag, add to the hot pan, and cook 4-5 minutes. Flip medallions, and cook another 4-5 minutes.

4. Add syrup to the pan, flipping the pork several times to coat. Remove from heat and serve immediately.

HELPFUL TIPS

Adding a pinch of dried sage to the rub will give these even more of a breakfast sausage taste that goes great with the syrup.

Bob's Crispy Iowa Pork Sandwich

prep time **15** mins · cook time **10** mins · serves **8** people · Bob Warden

I don't usually double dip, but when frying, I feel it's justified. Double breading makes for extra crunchy pork medallions to top these easy and delicious sandwiches.

1. Heat ½ inch of vegetable oil in large frying pan until 365 degrees.

2. In a mixing bowl, whisk together eggs and ¼ cup of tap water.

3. In another bowl, combine flour, cornmeal, thyme, salt, and pepper.

4. Dip pork slices in the egg mixture, then the flour mixture, then back into the egg, and then once more into the flour mixture.

5. Place breaded pork in the frying pan, frying until golden brown, about 3-4 minutes. Flip, and fry another 3-4 minutes. Transfer fried pork to paper towels to drain excess oil.

6. Split Kaiser rolls open and dress with lettuce, tomato, and honey mustard. Finish each sandwich with the fried slices of pork.

Shopping List

2 (**1 pound**) **pork tenderloins**, cut into ½ inch medallions

vegetable oil for frying

4 large eggs

2 cups **all purpose flour**

1 cup **yellow cornmeal**

1 teaspoon **dry thyme**

½ teaspoon **salt**

¼ teaspoon **pepper**

8 Kaiser rolls

green leaf lettuce

16 slices **tomato**

1 cup **honey mustard**

Helpful Tips

You can even use the eggs and flour to batter and fry the tomato slices to top the sandwich, something that we all know is great—especially if the tomatoes are green!

Tuscan Pork Tenderloin Stew

Tuscan Pork Tenderloin Stew

prep time **10** mins · cook time **30** mins · serves **8** people · Jan Muller

Although it is usually made from cornmeal, polenta can be made from several grains. I used to make my own polenta for this pork stew, but once when I was short on time, I brought the premade stuff home and it worked beautifully!

1. Add oil to a large sauté pan and heat on high.

2. Add pork strips to the hot oil and sauté until meat is browned and thoroughly cooked. Remove from pan and reserve.

3. Add green beans, onion, garlic, and mushrooms, sautéing until onions are soft.

4. Combine diced tomatoes with the cornstarch, add to the pan, and bring up to a simmer. Simmer until slightly thickened.

5. Add basil, oregano, and polenta to the pan and cook for 1 minute. Return pork to the pan and toss to coat.

Shopping List

2 (**1** pound) **pork tenderloins**, cut into strips

2 tablespoons **olive oil**

4 cups **green beans**, cleaned

1 **onion**, diced

1 clove **garlic**, minced

1 pound **mushrooms**, sliced

1 (**32**-ounce) can **diced tomatoes**, with juice

1 tablespoon **cornstarch**

1 tablespoon chopped **fresh basil**

1 teaspoon **fresh oregano leaves**

1 (**16**-ounce) tube **polenta**, sliced

salt and **pepper**

¼ cup shredded **Parmesan cheese**

6. Add salt and pepper to taste, and serve topped with shredded Parmesan cheese.

Helpful Tips

If you plan to make extra servings of this stew to vacuum seal and freeze, it is best to add the polenta right before serving rather before freezing. It simply does not freeze or reheat well.

PORK LOIN

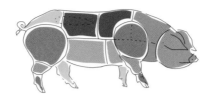

Most whole pork loins sold in bulk by warehouse clubs or in family packs at your local super market are boneless, and average about nine pounds each. They can usually be purchased at a savings of at least 50% when compared to the cost of smaller, individual roasts and packages of boneless pork chops. Vacuum sealed pork loins can usually be kept refrigerated for up to 10 days if purchased with a good 'sell by' date, or frozen for up to 1 year. If your pork loin is not vacuum sealed, you should divide and/or prepare it for storage within 2 or 3 days of purchase. Use a large chef's knife to divide your pork loin into roasts, chops, and stew meat.

A whole pork loin is usually around 5 inches in diameter by 18 inches long and is all but begging to be turned into juicy roasts. We recommend that you use at least a third of a whole loin as a roast. It will feed 4-6 people. Included in this section are 3 of our favorite recipes for pork loin roasts, as well as 4 delicious pork chop recipes.

When cutting chops from the loin, we recommend you cut the chops to your desired thickness, and then vacuum seal them in packs of 2-8 per package, depending upon the size of your family, and for what recipes you plan to use when preparing them. If you are planning on using a recipe that calls for a marinade, you can seal the marinade with the chops before you put them into storage. Then, when you need them, they are already marinated and ready to cook.

Pieces of the loin not used for roasts or chops

can be pre-cut into cubes for stew, or into strips for stir-fry, fajitas, and quesadillas. Stews can be made in advance, vacuum sealed, frozen, and then reheated by boiling in the bag with no fuss and no dirty pot.

CONTENTS

ROASTED PORK LOIN AND ROOT VEGETABLES

prep time **20** mins   cook time **3** hrs   serves **6** people   Bob Warden

SHOPPING LIST

I use parsnips, one of my favorite vegetables, in this easy to prepare dish. This marinated pork loin makes for a perfect comfort meal, and since you marinate it overnight, you'll have more time to prepare the perfect comfort dessert to go with it!

1. Combine olive oil, garlic, rosemary, and oregano to create a marinade. Seal pork loin and ½ of the marinade in a vacuum seal bag, and refrigerate for up to 24 hours. Reserve remaining marinade for later.

2. Preheat oven to 375 degrees.

3. Place potatoes, carrots, and parsnips in a large roasting pan, and pour reserved marinade over top.

1 boneless pork loin, about **3** pounds

½ cup **olive oil**

6 cloves **garlic**, minced

1 tablespoon minced **fresh rosemary**

½ teaspoon minced **fresh oregano**

4 potatoes, cut into wedges

4 carrots, cut into chunks

4 parsnips, cut into chunks

salt and **pepper**

4. Remove pork loin from marinade and place on top of vegetables. Generously season all with salt and pepper.

5. Bake 2 ½ to 3 hours. Remove from oven, let rest 15 minutes, and then slice. Serve with plenty of the root vegetables and smothered with juices from the pan.

HELPFUL TIPS

Out of one large pork loin you should be able to get two nice sized roasts for dinners. So that you'll already be prepared to make another recipe in this book, you can vacuum seal and freeze the other half of the pork loin whole or sliced into chops.

Curried Pork Chops

CURRIED PORK CHOPS

prep time **20** mins cook time **30** mins serves **6** people Jan Muller

Curry has found its way into many other cuisines beyond Indian. An important thing to remember is that not all curry powders are the same. Try different types until you find your favorite. Personally, my favorite is "Madras" curry powder.

SHOPPING LIST

6 pork chops cut from pork loin, ¾ inch thick

2 tablespoons **olive oil**

2 **onions**, diced

2 **apples**, cored and diced

1 (20-ounce) can **diced tomatoes**, with juice

½ cup **raisins**

2 ½ teaspoons **curry powder**

1 teaspoon **sugar**

¼ teaspoon **paprika**

salt and **pepper**

1. Add oil to a large sauté pan and heat on medium-high.

2. Add onions and apples to the hot oil, and sauté until soft. Remove from pan and reserve.

3. Add chops to the hot pan and cook 3 to 5 minutes to brown. Flip, and cook another 3 to 5 minutes. Remove from pan and reserve.

4. Add diced tomatoes with juice, raisins, curry powder, sugar, and paprika to the pan, and stir to combine. Bring up to a simmer, and then return the chops, onions, and apples to the pan.

5. Reduce heat just low enough to hold a simmer, cover pan, and let simmer for 10-15 minutes.

6. Season with salt and pepper to taste and serve chops smothered in the sauce, onions, apples, and raisins.

HELPFUL TIPS

The benefit of cutting your own pork chops from a pork loin is that they are guaranteed to be fresh, still moist, and just as thick as you want them to be.

Dried Fruit Stuffed Pork Loin

DRIED FRUIT STUFFED PORK LOIN

prep time **30** mins   cook time **2+** hrs   serves **6** people   Bob Warden

Dried fruits are perfect for stuffing because they soak up all the good juices from the roast and plump up while cooking. This roast takes a little bit of effort, but slices up into the most beautiful presentation.

1. Preheat oven to 350 degrees. Place olive oil and garlic in a sauté pan, heat on medium-high, and sauté until garlic is soft.

2. In a mixing bowl, combine 2 tablespoons of the softened garlic with the rosemary, apricots, cranberries, and ½ cup of the apple jelly to create the stuffing.

3. Butterfly the pork loin by slicing into it lengthwise, almost all the way through to the other side. Unfold and you should have two halves, still connected in the middle.

4. Rub the pork loin inside and out with the remaining cooked garlic in oil. Generously season with salt and pepper.

SHOPPING LIST

1 boneless pork loin, about **3** pounds

3 tablespoons **olive oil**

16 cloves **garlic**, minced

3 tablespoons minced **fresh rosemary**

16 dried apricots, chopped

⅓ cup **dried cranberries**

1 cup **apple jelly**

salt and **pepper**

twine

¼ cup **brandy**

½ cup **chicken broth** or **stock**

5. Evenly distribute the stuffing inside the pork loin, fold to close, and tie in several spots with twine to hold together. Bake on a sheet pan for 2 hours.

6. Remove roast from oven and raise oven temperature to 400 degrees. Brush the remaining ½ cup of apple jelly over the roast, and bake an additional 20 minutes.

7. Transfer roast to a cutting board and let rest for 15 minutes. Meanwhile, pour any pan juices, the brandy, and the chicken broth into a saucepot and heat on medium-high, bringing to a boil. Slice roast and serve smothered in the sauce from the saucepot.

HELPFUL TIPS

With a recipe as intricate as this one, it is always a good idea to stuff two pork loins, vacuum sealing and freezing the second. This will save a ton of prep time when you want to prepare this dish again.

SOUTHERN FRIED PORK CHOPS WITH BACON GRAVY

prep time **10** mins   cook time **30** mins   serves **6** people   Bob Warden

Fried foods are legendary in the south. Lots of home cooks stake their reputations on their fried chicken, and I will stake mine on these fried pork chops. Chicken broth, bacon, and onions help to create a gravy that never disappoints.

SHOPPING LIST

6 pork chops cut from pork loin, ¾ inch thick

6 slices **bacon**

4 tablespoons **butter**

1 onion, diced

1 ½ cups **chicken broth** or **stock**

¼ cup **cornstarch**

salt and **pepper**

1. Place bacon in a large sauté pan and heat on medium-high. Cook until crispy, remove, chop, and reserve.

2. Add 2 tablespoons of the butter to the hot bacon grease in the pan, and sauté onions until soft. Remove from pan and reserve.

3. Add chops to the hot pan, and sauté 3 to 5 minutes. Flip chops, sauté for another 3 to 5 minutes, and return bacon and onions to pan.

4. Add chicken broth and the 2 remaining tablespoons of butter to the pan, cover, and simmer 5 to 10 minutes. Remove chops and cover them with aluminum foil to keep warm.

5. Mix cornstarch into ¼ cup of tap water, and then whisk into the juices in the pan. Bring up to a simmer, and simmer until thickened.

6. Season with salt and pepper to taste. Serve chops smothered in gravy.

HELPFUL TIPS

If you are vacuum sealing and freezing extra chops cut from the whole pork loin, pierce the chops repeatedly with a fork to help tenderize the meat before freezing.

PORK CHOPS WITH CARAMELIZED APPLES AND ONIONS

prep time **20** mins   cook time **25** mins   serves **6** people   Jan Muller

With this apple and onion pairing, you will never have to eat disappointingly dry pork chops again. My mother used to whip up this dish for our annual family reunions, which may explain why they were always so well attended.

1. Place 2 tablespoons of the butter in a large sauté pan and heat medium-high.

2. Place chops in the hot pan and cook 3 to 4 minutes. Flip chops, and cook for another 3 to 4 minutes. Remove from pan and reserve.

3. Place the remaining 2 tablespoons of butter in pan and add the onions, sautéing until almost soft.

4. Add the brown sugar, cinnamon, nutmeg, garlic, and apples to the pan and continue sautéing until apples are soft.

5. Add chicken broth and bring to a simmer.

6. Return chops to the pan, cover, and cook 5 to 7 minutes to reheat chops. Serve topped with apples, onions, and juices from the pan. Garnish with roasted pecans.

SHOPPING LIST

6 pork chops cut from pork loin, ¾ inch thick

4 tablespoons **butter**

2 onions, sliced thinly

3 tablespoons **light brown sugar**

¼ teaspoon **ground cinnamon**

¼ teaspoon **nutmeg**

1 clove **garlic,** minced

3 Granny Smith apples, cored and sliced thin

½ cup **chicken broth** or **stock**

¼ cup **roasted pecans**

HELPFUL TIPS

While you can purchase already roasted pecans for this recipe, I like to roast my own pecans by heating them in a dry sauté pan over medium heat until they are fragrant and slightly more crunchy.

Cranberry Glazed Pork Loin Roast

CRANBERRY GLAZED PORK LOIN ROAST

prep time **15** mins | cook time **1** hour | serves **10** people | Bob Warden

Believing in serving more than just turkey, this is one of several pork loin recipes my grandmother would consider for our Thanksgiving dinners. I also often serve this for Christmas dinner, because it is so pretty and festive, especially if you garnish it with a few fresh cranberries.

SHOPPING LIST

1 **boneless pork loin**, about **3** pounds

2 cups **chicken broth**

1 (**14.5**-ounce) can **whole-berry cranberry sauce**

1 cup **apple jelly**

1 tablespoon **Dijon mustard**

1 teaspoon **horseradish**

2 teaspoons **granulated garlic**

1 teaspoon **dry thyme**

1 teaspoon **dry sage**

salt and **pepper**

1. Preheat oven to 425 degrees.

2. Place chicken broth in a saucepot and heat on high, boiling until the liquid is reduced by half.

3. Add cranberry sauce, apple jelly, mustard, horseradish, garlic, thyme, and sage to the pot, and bring back up to a boil. Stir until well combined.

4. Generously season pork loin with salt and pepper, and place in a roasting pan. Pour sauce over top loin.

5. Bake 1 hour, frequently basting with the sauce.

6. Let rest 15 minutes before slicing and serving drizzled with the sauce from the roasting pan.

HELPFUL TIPS

Frequent basting will not only give this roast more flavor, but also a really nice color for a nice presentation. Leftover sauce from the pan can be used as a marinade by vacuum sealing it along with raw pork chops.

GRILLED BOURBON BROWN SUGAR PORK CHOPS

prep time **15** mins cook time **18** mins serves **8** people Jan Muller

These tender pork chops and their overnight bourbon marinade grill up beautifully caramelized thanks to a little bit of brown sugar. The bourbon cooks out as it grills, but leaves behind a really great flavor that lends itself well to the pork.

1. Whisk together all marinade ingredients. Seal marinade and chops in a vacuum seal bag and refrigerate for up to 24 hours.

2. Lightly oil or spray a grill or indoor grill pan, and then heat on high.

3. Remove chops from the marinade and let rest 15 minutes. Discard marinade.

4. Place chops on grill or grill pan, and grill for 5 to 7 minutes. Flip chops, and grill for 5 to 7 additional minutes.

5. Transfer to a cooler part of the grill, and grill for an additional 2 to 4 minutes. Serve immediately.

SHOPPING LIST

8 pork chops cut from pork loin, ¾ inch thick

MARINADE

¾ cup **soy sauce**, regular or reduced sodium

½ cup **bourbon**

¼ cup **Worcestershire sauce**

¼ cup **chicken broth** or **stock**

¼ cup **olive oil**

2 tablespoons **minced garlic**

1 ½ teaspoons **Dijon mustard**

3 tablespoons **light brown sugar**

HELPFUL TIPS

During the summer, add some peaches tossed with brown sugar to the grill with the pork chops and serve together! All you need to do is sear the peaches on the grill just long enough that they're marked.

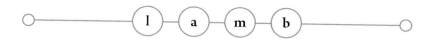
RACK OF LAMB

Lamb has become more and more popular as its availability has increased. Rack of lamb is pretty much everyone's favorite cut of lamb. It is also the most expensive cut, so if you like rack of lamb, it is really important to buy it in bulk. You can typically save 30-40% on rack of lamb at a warehouse club over traditional grocery stores.

The real beauty of warehouse club rack of lamb is that it almost always comes pre-vacuum sealed—and even better—they also come pre-Frenched and ready to roast.

What is 'Frenched?' Frenching is the time consuming process of cutting and scraping away the bottom couple of inches of fat from the whole rib rack. Properly done, the end of the bones will be perfectly clean, thereby becoming a handle that can turn individual rib pieces into mouth watering finger-food. I don't know anyone that does not lick these bones clean.

A full rack will consist of eight bones, and typically serves two people. Vacuum sealed lamb can be stored for up to a week in the refrigerator or up to six months in the freezer. We usually do nothing to the racks until we are ready to cook them. Most of the time, we are simply seasoning them.

Rosemary is lamb's best friend, and a few sprigs in the roasting pan will help bring out the best in lamb. Like pork tenderloins, rack of lamb is also delicious accompanied with a fruit jelly. But, of course it is mint jelly that has a very special affinity for lamb.

Individual lamb chops cut from the whole rack marinate very quickly, so we usually do that just before cooking.

When the individual ribs are cut prior to cooking, we also like breading them with a variety of flavored crumbs. In the recipes that follow, you'll find a pretty incredible recipe for lamb chops breaded in pistachio crumbs!

CONTENTS

QUICK GRILLED LAMB CHOPS

prep time **10** mins cook time **12** mins serves **6** people Bob Warden

Not only is this one of my go-to marinades when I do not have a lot of time to make one up, but in the summer when I am invited to a cook out, I bring a bottle of this marinade as a host gift. It works great on vegetables too, though I usually add a squeeze of lemon.

SHOPPING LIST

12 lamb chops

¼ cup **white vinegar**

2 tablespoons **olive oil**

1 tablespoon **minced garlic**

1 onion, chopped

2 teaspoons minced **fresh rosemary**

2 teaspoons minced **fresh tarragon**

salt and **pepper**

1. Combine white vinegar, olive oil, garlic, onion, rosemary, and tarragon to create a marinade. Seal marinade and lamb chops in a vacuum seal bag, and refrigerate for up to 24 hours.

2. Oil or spray a grill or indoor grill pan and heat on high.

3. Remove lamb chops from marinade and generously season with salt and pepper.

4. Place lamb chops on the hot grill, grill for 4 to 6 minutes, flip, and grill for another 4 to 6 minutes for medium doneness. Serve immediately.

HELPFUL TIPS

Switch out the white vinegar with balsamic vinegar for more of a tangy flavor. Remember, with marinades, the longer the meat sits in the marinade the more tender and more infused with flavor it gets.

ASIAN CONTINENTAL LAMB CHOPS

prep time **10** mins — cook time **16** mins — serves **6** people — Jan Muller

Many people think of lamb as very gamey tasting, oftentimes because they have only had leg of lamb, which does tend to have a stronger flavor than rack of lamb. Regardless of the reason, I know not everyone likes lamb, but when I serve it with this combination of ingredients everyone seems to love it.

1. In a mixing bowl, combine red wine, soy sauce, mint, basil, garlic, and ginger. Seal mixture in a vacuum seal bag along with lamb chops, and marinate in refrigerator for up to 24 hours.

2. Place oven rack in its highest position and preheat broiler.

SHOPPING LIST

12 lamb chops

¾ cup **red wine**

¼ cup **soy sauce**, regular or reduced sodium

1 tablespoon minced **fresh mint**

1 tablespoon minced **fresh basil**

2 cloves **garlic**, minced

½ teaspoon minced **fresh ginger**

salt and **pepper**

3. Remove lamb from the marinade, let rest 15 minutes, and generously season with salt and pepper.

4. Place lamb on a broiler pan and broil for 6 to 8 minutes, flip, and broil for another 6 to 8 minutes for medium doneness. Serve immediately.

HELPFUL TIPS

Feel free to experiment with different Asian sauces, such as teriyaki or hoisin sauce instead of the soy sauce to change things up.

Lamb Chops with Mint Pistachio Paste

l a m b

LAMB CHOPS WITH MINT PISTACHIO PASTE

prep time **15** mins   cook time **25** mins   serves **4** people   Jan Muller

Personally, I was never a fan of mint jelly, but I still wanted to incorporate mint flavor into my lamb. This paste ended up being the way to go. You will be pleasantly surprised at how nice the lamb tastes with pistachios, but if you are using salted pistachios, you can probably skip the salt in this recipe.

1. Preheat oven to 375 degrees.

2. Add oil to a large sauté pan over medium-high heat.

3. In a food processor, pulse together the pistachios, peppercorns, garlic, mint, marjoram, and mustard.

4. Generously season chops with salt, and then spread pistachio paste on one side of each lamb chop.

5. Add lamb chops to the hot pan, sauté for 2 to 3 minutes to brown, flip chops, and sauté another 2 to 3 minutes to brown on the other side.

6. Transfer chops to a baking dish, place in oven, and bake for 15 to 20 minutes for medium doneness. Serve immediately.

SHOPPING LIST

8 lamb chops

2 tablespoons **olive oil**

1 cup **shelled pistachios**

2 tablespoons **crushed black peppercorns**

2 tablespoons **minced garlic**

1 tablespoon minced **fresh mint**

1 tablespoon minced **fresh marjoram**

¼ cup **mustard**

salt

HELPFUL TIPS

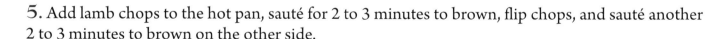

The paste can be made in large quantities and vacuum sealed to last longer. Also, cracked black pepper can be substituted for crushed black pepper.

DIJON CRUSTED LAMB CHOPS

prep time **10** mins　　cook time **16** mins　　serves **6** people　　Bob Warden

Mustard does a wonderful job of keeping the crust on these chops held firmly in place. It's just about the tastiest glue you can find in your kitchen! If you like your lamb chops cooked more on the well done side, turn the oven down to 375 degrees and move the chops to a lower shelf in the oven to finish cooking, so you do not burn your crust.

SHOPPING LIST

12 lamb chops

1 cup **breadcrumbs**

4 cloves **garlic**, crushed

2 teaspoons **dry thyme**

¾ cup **Dijon mustard**

salt and **pepper**

1. Place oven rack in its highest position and preheat broiler.

2. Combine breadcrumbs, garlic, thyme, and ½ cup of the mustard to create a paste.

3. Brush chops with remaining ¼ cup mustard and generously season with salt and pepper.

4. Spread paste onto one or both sides of each lamb chop.

5. Place lamb chops on a broiler pan and place under broiler for 6 to 8 minutes, flip chops, and broil for another 6 to 8 minutes for medium doneness. Serve immediately.

HELPFUL TIPS

Even breadcrumbs get stale, so remember to vacuum seal for freshness, especially if you make your own. Though you usually make breadcrumbs from bread that is going stale in the first place, you don't need it getting any staler!

Tilapia

Warehouse clubs usually have a good variety of bulk packaged fish fillets, such as tilapia, a very mild white fish. The savings on bulk packaged fillets is usually around 30% versus grocery stores that only offer smaller, 4-6 fillet packs.

Because fish fillets are very perishable, you will need to repackage your fillets into smaller batches appropriate to the size of your family, and then vacuum seal them for long term freezing.

If you don't own a vacuum sealer, get all of the air that you can out of your freezer bag with a straw. About one month will be maximum storage time if your tilapia fillets are not properly vacuum sealed before freezing.

If recipes call for breading the tilapia, you can go ahead and bread them when you get them home, and then put the breaded fillets into your vacuum sealer bags. We have found through experience that it is best to put the tilapia fillets onto a wax paper lined tray and freeze them for several hours before finally packaging for long term storage. This prevents the fillets from sticking together, and allows you to remove only what you need from the bag without having to wait until all fillets have defrosted. Tilapia can be cooked straight from the frozen fillets, simply by doubling the cooking time.

While Bob's Broiled Tilapia with Cherry Tomato Relish is a delicious dish with a colorful presentation, Jan's Fish Tacos with Lime Dressing really steal the show in this category!

CONTENTS

Broiled Tilapia with Cherry Tomato Relish

BROILED TILAPIA WITH CHERRY TOMATO RELISH

prep time **55** mins   cook time **10** mins   serves **8** people   Bob Warden

I find that the tried and true combination of basil and lemon in this recipe enhances the flavor of tilapia, while the crunchy Parmesan cheese topping adds an interesting texture. This dish works well with most mild fish, so if you have caught your own, and it is not tilapia, feel free to substitute.

1. Combine the ¼ cup olive oil, lemon juice, basil, and pepper to create a marinade. Place tilapia in a vacuum seal bag, cover with marinade, and seal. Refrigerate for 2 hours.

2. Place oven rack at the highest position and preheat broiler.

3. Meanwhile, add the 2 tablespoons of olive oil to a large sauté pan and heat on medium-high.

4. Add tomatoes, onion, and celery to the hot pan and sauté until softened. Remove from heat and set aside.

SHOPPING LIST

8 tilapia fillets

¼ cup **olive oil**

2 tablespoons **lemon juice**

¼ teaspoon minced **fresh basil**

¼ teaspoon **pepper**

2 tablespoons **olive oil**

1 pint **cherry tomatoes**, halved

1 cup chopped **onion**

1 cup chopped **celery**

salt and **pepper**

½ cup grated **Parmesan cheese**

5. Remove fillets from marinade and arrange on a broiler pan. Arrange sautéed tomato mixture around fillets, and lightly season all with salt and pepper. Broil for 5 minutes.

6. Remove from the oven and cover fillets with the Parmesan cheese. Broil for 2 additional minutes or until the topping is browned and the fish flakes easily with a fork.

HELPFUL TIPS

Try varying the relish ingredients by adding diced red and green bell peppers and minced garlic for a little extra zing.

GRILLED TILAPIA WITH ISLAND SALSA

prep time **45** mins   cook time **10** mins   serves **6** people   Bob Warden

I love this recipe because, though it may seem like a lot of ingredients, it is super easy to make, and the salsa can be made a day ahead to really let the flavors come together. If you do make the salsa a day ahead, you should vacuum seal it to keep the avocado nice and green.

1. Combine all marinade ingredients and seal along with tilapia in a vacuum seal bag. Refrigerate for 2 hours.

2. Meanwhile, combine all Island Salsa ingredients. Refrigerate until ready to serve.

3. Lightly oil a grill or indoor grill pan and heat on high.

4. Remove tilapia fillets from marinade and let rest 15 minutes. Season lightly with salt and pepper. Discard the remaining marinade.

5. Place fillets on grill, grill for 4 to 5 minutes, flip, and grill for another 4 to 5 minutes. Serve topped with the Island Salsa.

SHOPPING LIST

6 tilapia fillets

MARINADE

1 cup **olive oil**

3 tablespoons **lemon juice**

3 tablespoons **lime juice**

3 tablespoons **orange juice**

1 clove **garlic**, minced

ISLAND SALSA

1 **mango**, pitted, peeled, and diced

1 **avocado**, pitted, peeled, and diced

1 tablespoon chopped **fresh cilantro**

2 tablespoons **lime juice**

1 tablespoon **lemon juice**

salt and **pepper**

HELPFUL TIPS

If you have leftover salsa, try combining it with black beans and cut and cleaned romaine lettuce to make a nice salad.

SIMPLE RANCHY BREADED FISH FILLETS

prep time **15** mins · cook time **10** mins · serves **4** people · Jan Muller

I enjoy making this meal for my family, as it is quick and easy to prepare with just a few ingredients. Sometimes for the kids, I cut the fish into sticks before breading, and serve them with French fries and coleslaw. It's a nice escape from the fast food alternatives that use minced pieces of fish in place of the whole fillets in this recipe.

SHOPPING LIST

4 tilapia fillets

¾ cup **Italian breadcrumbs**

1 (1-ounce) packet **Ranch dressing mix**

2 eggs, beaten

1 tablespoon **butter**

1 tablespoon **vegetable oil**

1. Mix together breadcrumbs and ranch dressing.

2. Dip tilapia in egg, and then dredge in the breadcrumb mixture to lightly coat fillets.

3. Add butter and vegetable oil to a large sauté pan and heat on medium heat until sizzling.

4. Place breaded tilapia in the hot pan, sauté for 3 to 5 minutes until golden brown, flip, and sauté for another 3 to 5 minutes on the other side.

5. Serve immediately.

HELPFUL TIPS

Experiment with other dry dressing mixes to add a little variety for your family. Bread up your fish, vacuum seal, and freeze it for a quick meal in the middle of the week.

Fish Tacos with Lime Dressing

FISH TACOS WITH LIME DRESSING

prep time **35** mins · cook time **6** mins · serves **6** people · Jan Muller

Fish tacos are a great change of pace from the everyday ground beef tacos that we've all been eating for years. Coincidentally, these tacos are also a great change of pace from the more everyday fish fillet preparations! You can also try adding your favorite guacamole or using a fresh tomato salsa in place of the diced tomatoes and cilantro.

SHOPPING LIST

1 pound **tilapia fillets**, cut into chunks
½ cup **olive oil**
2 tablespoons **white vinegar**
4 tablespoons **fresh lime juice**
4 teaspoons **lime zest**
1 ½ teaspoons **honey**
2 cloves **garlic**, minced
½ teaspoon **cumin**
½ teaspoon **chili powder**
1 cup **sour cream**
⅛ teaspoon **cumin**
⅛ teaspoon **coriander**
¼ teaspoon **chili powder**
½ teaspoon **Old Bay seasoning**
2 tablespoons **olive oil**
salt and **pepper**
1 package **taco shells** (**12** shells)
3 ripe **tomatoes**, diced
1 bunch **cilantro**, chopped
1 head **iceberg lettuce**, shredded

1. Whisk together the ½ cup olive oil, white vinegar, 2 tablespoons of the lime juice, 2 teaspoons of the lime zest, honey, garlic, the ½ teaspoon cumin, and the ½ teaspoon chili powder to create a marinade. Place tilapia into a vacuum seal bag, cover with marinade, and seal. Refrigerate for 2 hours.

2. Meanwhile, make the dressing by whisking together the sour cream, the remaining 2 tablespoons of lime juice and lime zest, the ⅛ teaspoon cumin, coriander, the ¼ teaspoon chili powder, and Old Bay seasoning. Refrigerate until needed.

3. Add the 2 tablespoons of olive oil to a large sauté pan over high heat.

4. Remove fish from marinade, place in the hot pan, and season lightly with salt and pepper. Sauté for 4-6 minutes, stirring occasionally, until fish is white throughout.

5. Assemble tacos by placing a portion of the fish pieces in the center of each taco shell with desired amount of tomatoes, cilantro, and lettuce. Drizzle with dressing and serve.

HELPFUL TIPS

The marinated fish in this recipe can also be baked in the oven. Heat oven to 350 degrees, place fish in a baking dish, and bake in the oven for 9 to 11 minutes.

LEMON DILL TILAPIA

prep time (10) mins   cook time (30) mins   serves (4) people   Bob Warden

Baked tilapia is a healthy choice that is easy to prepare. I think fresh asparagus makes a nice addition to this dish; just place the asparagus in the baking dish underneath the fish fillets and they will both roast within the allowed time.

SHOPPING LIST

4 tilapia fillets

3 tablespoons lemon juice

1 tablespoon olive oil

1 clove garlic, chopped

1 teaspoon chopped fresh dill

nonstick cooking spray

salt and pepper

1. Whisk together lemon juice, olive oil, garlic, and dill to create a marinade. Place tilapia fillets into a vacuum seal bag, cover with marinade, and seal. Refrigerate for 2 hours.

2. Preheat oven to 375 degrees and spray a baking dish with nonstick cooking spray.

3. Remove fillets from marinade and place in baking dish, pouring marinade over top. Season lightly with salt and pepper.

4. Bake for 25 to 30 minutes, until fish is flaky and white throughout. Serve immediately.

HELPFUL TIPS

For an extra fresh flavor, substitute fresh lemon juice for bottled, and then you can also zest the lemons and add a pinch of the zest to the marinade. Though I keep a bottle of lemon juice in my fridge as a backup, I almost always go for the fuller taste of fresh when available.

SALMON

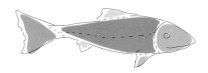

Salmon is available in bulk, and in several different ways, in most warehouse clubs. In season, it is often available fresh-frozen and whole. This will always be the lowest priced option, but whole salmon is not always available, and does require butchering, unless you are going to roast a whole salmon for a crowd (they would love it)! We usually buy the vacuum packed whole fillets of salmon. These typically weigh in around 3 pounds or more, so you usually have enough fish to make two complete meals.

The typical savings on salmon is going to be around 40-50% versus individually packed salmon fillets or steaks in the supermarket. We bring home the whole fillet, open it, and cut into 4 to 6 ounce pieces. These are then vacuum sealed in dinner-ready groupings and placed into the freezer for storage.

It is best to thoroughly dry the salmon with a paper towel before putting them into freezer or vacuum sealing bags. You can also freeze the pieces on a wax paper lined tray for just a few hours before vacuum sealing to keep the individual fillets from sticking together as they freeze. This will also cut down on your thawing time.

We love salmon for its rich, oily texture and distinct flavor. It is, without a doubt, our favorite fish. Salmon is great broiled, sautéed, grilled, and even poached with only salt and pepper.

Where salmon really shines is with a variety of herbs and spices. We especially like 'salmon seasoning' available at most fish counters.

Like most fish, salmon goes great with lemon, and we almost always squeeze some lemon juice onto it before, and after cooking. Poached salmon is also great in salads. The recipes in this section are just a few of our favorites, but we could write an entire book on the lovely creature. We are, however, still waiting for all of salmon's skin-friendly omega-3 fatty acids to take us back to how we looked in the 1980s!

CONTENTS

Lemon Tarragon Baked Salmon

LEMON TARRAGON BAKED SALMON

prep time **15** mins · cook time **25** mins · serves **6** people · Bob Warden

The acidity of lemon does a great job of counteracting the (good) fattiness of salmon. Adding lemon zest to the marinade in this recipe gives the dish a big boost of lemon flavor that you just can't get with juice alone.

1. Whisk together garlic, olive oil, tarragon, basil, lemon juice, and lemon zest to create a marinade. Seal the marinade and salmon in a vacuum seal bag and let marinate in refrigerator for up to 4 hours.

2. Preheat oven to 375 degrees.

3. Remove salmon from the marinade, place in a baking dish, pour marinade over salmon, and then lightly season with salt and pepper. Place in oven and bake 20 to 25 minutes. Serve immediately.

SHOPPING LIST

6 (6-ounce) **salmon fillets**

4 cloves **garlic**, minced

½ cup **olive oil**

2 tablespoons minced **fresh tarragon**

2 tablespoons minced **fresh basil**

2 **lemons**, juiced and zested

salt and **pepper**

HELPFUL TIPS

I prep double of the basil, tarragon, and lemon, and add the extra to steamed white rice to serve alongside the salmon, which makes for a nice light meal.

SWEET GINGER GRILLED SALMON

prep time **10** mins cook time **14** mins serves **6** people Jan Muller

This salmon with a sweet ginger marinade is one of the main features of our summer grilling on the deck as it is so easy and so satisfying! I keep vacuum sealed bags of this salmon in my freezer. That way I can thaw overnight in my refrigerator and I am grilling in no time.

SHOPPING LIST

6 (6-ounce) **salmon fillets**

1 cup **soy sauce**, regular or reduced sodium

1 cup **light brown sugar**

2 teaspoons minced **fresh ginger**

2 cloves **garlic**, minced

¼ cup **olive oil**

1. Whisk together soy sauce, brown sugar, ginger, garlic, and olive oil to create a marinade. Seal marinade and salmon in a vacuum seal bag. Refrigerate for up to 4 hours.

2. Lightly oil or spray a grill or indoor grill pan, and then heat on medium-high.

3. Remove salmon from marinade and let rest 15 minutes, discarding marinade.

4. Place salmon on grill, grill 5 to 7 minutes, flip, and grill for another 5 to 7 minutes. Serve immediately.

HELPFUL TIPS

You can save the marinade to brush the salmon with after flipping on the grill. You'll get an even better glaze on the salmon this way, but watch out for the oil in the marinade dripping into the flames and flaring up!

Greek Summer Salad with Broiled Salmon

prep time **25** mins   cook time **14** mins   serves **6** people   Jan Muller

I love this salmon and salad duet! With feta cheese, black olives, cucumber, red onion, and oregano, it has a great combination of Greek flavors that work surprisingly well with salmon. Great for lunch, but hearty enough for a dinner, I'll eat it anytime!

1. Whisk together olive oil, cumin, paprika, and orange juice to create a marinade. Seal marinade and salmon in a vacuum seal bag and refrigerate for up to 4 hours.

2. Place oven rack at the highest position and preheat broiler.

3. Remove salmon from marinade, place on broiler pan, and season lightly with salt and pepper. Discard marinade.

4. Place salmon under broiler, broil 5 to 7 minutes, flip, and broil for another 5 to 7 minutes.

Shopping List

6 (6-ounce) **salmon fillets**

⅛ cup **olive oil**

2 tablespoons **cumin**

2 teaspoons **paprika**

¼ cup **orange juice**

salt and **pepper**

Salad

6 cups chopped **romaine lettuce**

1 (6-ounce) can **black olives**, drained

3 **scallions**, chopped

1 cup **crumbled feta cheese**

1 **cucumber**, diced

1 **red onion**, sliced thinly

1 teaspoon chopped **fresh oregano**

1 cup **garlic salad dressing** (can use Greek)

5. Meanwhile, in a large bowl, toss all salad ingredients, coating everything equally with salad dressing. Divide equally among 6 plates.

6. Remove salmon from broiler, place a salmon fillet on top of each salad, and serve immediately.

Helpful Tips

You can also grill the salmon. If you do, marinate the red onions with the salmon and grill the marinated onions to top the salad as well.

Steamed Salmon with Mustard Glaze and Peach Chutney

STEAMED SALMON WITH MUSTARD GLAZE AND PEACH CHUTNEY

prep time **10** mins   cook time **10** mins   serves **6** people   Jan Muller

Lime juice and mustard alone always adds zest to salmon, but I love the addition of the peach chutney topping as it really takes this salmon to a whole new level. If you want to spice up the chutney, you can add some red pepper flakes to it. I like to garnish with a fresh sprig of cilantro.

1. In a steamer, bring 1 inch of water to a boil.

2. Lightly season salmon with salt and pepper, place on rack in steamer, cover, and steam 8 to 10 minutes.

3. Meanwhile, add all chutney ingredients to a saucepan and heat over medium heat, simmering until peaches are soft and liquids thicken.

4. In a mixing bowl, whisk together all mustard glaze ingredients.

5. Remove salmon from steamer and serve each fillet smothered with mustard glaze and topped with a spoonful of peach chutney.

SHOPPING LIST

6 (6-ounce) **salmon fillets**

salt and **pepper**

PEACH CHUTNEY

4 peaches, pitted and diced

1 green bell pepper, diced

½ **onion**, diced

½ cup **cider vinegar**

¼ cup **light brown sugar**

MUSTARD GLAZE

¼ cup **lime juice**

2 tablespoons **olive oil**

1 tablespoon **Dijon mustard**

⅛ teaspoon **ground ginger**

⅛ teaspoon **garlic powder**

HELPFUL TIPS

You can also use the glaze as a marinade. Simply vacuum seal it with the salmon and marinate for at least 1 hour in the refrigerator. If marinating, I'd suggest grilling rather than steaming to really brown the marinade.

seafood

BASIL TOMATO ROASTED SALMON

prep time **10** mins   cook time **20** mins   serves **6** people   Bob Warden

Salmon is rich in Omega-3's, so I am always looking for new and better ways to eat more of it. This recipe has a basil mayonnaise sauce baked atop fresh tomatoes stacked atop the salmon. It's definitely something new and I like to think that it is definitely something better than ordinary.

1. Preheat oven to 425 degrees.

2. In a bowl, combine basil and mayonnaise.

3. Lightly season salmon with salt and pepper, place into a baking dish, and top each fillet with 2 slices of tomato. Top tomato slices with a portion of the mayonnaise mixture.

4. Bake 15 to 20 minutes and serve garnished with basil leaves.

SHOPPING LIST

6 (6-ounce) **salmon fillets**

3 tablespoons chopped **fresh basil**

1 ½ cups **mayonnaise**

salt and **pepper**

12 slices **tomato**

6 **basil leaves**, for garnish

HELPFUL TIPS

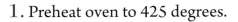

Tomatoes and basil of course work great together, but try experimenting with other herbs to use in the mayonnaise, such as dill or tarragon. Buy sides of salmon to save money, and then cut into 6 ounce portions, vacuum seal, and freeze so that you have it on hand.

JAN MULLER

With over 30 years in the Housewares Industry, **Jan Muller** is a well recognized television demonstrator, and frequent QVC on-air guest. With Bob, Jan helped develop Nationwide Marketing Inc, the original marketers of the FoodSaver® vacuum sealing system. Jan's passion for cooking led him to an internship with L'École des Chefs where he studied under the expertise of Chefs Thomas Keller and Eric Ripert. In 2002, Jan authored his first cookbook, *Simple Feasts: The Cookbook for the Seasons*.

BOB WARDEN

With forty years experience as a chef, restaurant owner, television personality, and kitchenware product developer, **Bob Warden** is now best known as an on air presenter at QVC. Over the years, Bob has helped develop over 1,000 kitchen products for the network. With Jan, Bob helped develop Nationwide Marketing Inc, the original marketers of the FoodSaver® vacuum sealing system. This is his seventh cookbook. His previous cookbooks include *Bob Warden's Slow Food Fast*, and *Bob Warden's Ninja Master Prep Cookbook*.

RECISE INDEX

CONTINUED ON NEXT PAGE...

PUBLISHER'S NOTE

This book is designed to be used in your kitchen. The pages lay flat and have been sewn together for extra durability. Feel free to fold this book open on your countertop to follow along with any recipe.